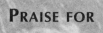

Praise for

Reap The Harvest

"This book is MUST reading for every pastor with even a distant interest in cell groups! I should know. For the past 23 years, I have spoken and consulted with hundreds of cell churches. In this single volume, Dr. Comiskey traces the biblical and historical basis of groups, explains prevalent types of group systems, and gives practical insights and principles for workable transition to become an effective cell church."

KAREN HURSTON
Hurston Ministries

"*Reap the Harvest* contains valuable insights for anyone committed to building a balanced, healthy, cell-based church according to the New Testament pattern."

LARRY KREIDER
International Director, DOVE Christian Fellowship International

"If you want to 'convert pew-sitters into pastors,' read this book. Joel Comiskey compares and defines the different small group-based models and presents the cell church as the champion of church-growth concepts around the world. He shows us how every member of the Body of Christ can 'experience the true church in a dynamic way.'"

BILLY HORNSBY
National Director, Bethany Cell Church Network

"Absolutely mandatory reading if you are serious about doing church as it is outlined in the New Testament. Thanks, Joel, for this good work."
BOB DAVIS
Senior Pastor, Long Reach Church of God

"I am really excited about *Reap the Harvest*. Joel Comiskey knows the proven principles of successful cell ministry. He traveled the world to discover them and then tested them in the crucible of his experience. This book offers the practical insights that turn the promise of cell ministry into a dynamic reality."
JIM EGLI
Director of Training, TOUCH Outreach Ministries

"This on-target book will help you learn from some of the most successful small-group ministries in the world and give you a clear focus on the system that you need to develop in your church to be producing small groups and multiplying your ministry and outreach. Few people like Joel Comiskey understand the importance of putting in place a workable system for small-group ministry in order to get results that you are after. This book is a key to helping you put purpose into your small groups and get the results that you are after."
DALE E. GALLOWAY
Dean, The Beeson International Center

"So many churches go for decades unable to break the "200 barrier" ... or fulfill their potential. One reason is that they lack infrastructure to grow. *Reap the Harvest* is an excellent 'how-to-get-it-done' guide for cell-group life with a purpose: the harvest. The chapter on change alone is worth the whole book! This is a practical, powerful, and useful tool that will save you from the common mistakes and guide you to healthy, vital quality and quantity growth."

KENT R. HUNTER
The Church Doctor

"Most books on cell groups are narrowly focused. In many of them, the author's purpose seems to be to convince the reader that their system is the best. This book is different! In it, Joel Comiskey gives us the broad picture in a concise and understandable way. You will be able to see clearly the strengths and weaknesses of many different approaches, and then decide which one might be the best for you."

C. PETER WAGNER
Chancellor, Wagner Leadership Institute

"I would love to visit some of the fastest growing cell churches around the world. But, like most pastors, I do not have the money or time. Joel Comiskey has done the traveling and research and has written a resource for the rest of us. His combination of thorough research and practical application makes this resource a must-read for any pastor or team planting or transitioning to a cell church."

MICHAEL MACK
The Small Group Network

"Once again, Dr. Joel Comiskey has written a most useful book for those interested in the use of small groups as a means of evangelism. I appreciate the balance of this book: with its focus on both growth in numbers and growth in depth. This is a mature reflection on the world-wide small group movement that builds on what others have discovered but then goes beyond this to fresh insights."

RICHARD PEACE
Professor, Fuller Theological Seminary

REAP THE HARVEST

REAP THE HARVEST

HOW A SMALL-GROUP SYSTEM CAN GROW YOUR CHURCH

JOEL COMISKEY

TOUCH PUBLICATIONS

Houston, Texas, U.S.A.

Published by TOUCH Publications
P.O. Box 19888
Houston, Texas, 77224-9888, U.S.A.
(281) 497-7901 • Fax (281) 497-0904

Jacket design by Don Bleyl
Text design by Rick Chandler
Editing by Scott Boren and Elizabeth Bruns

International Standard Book Number: 1-880828-13-8

TOUCH Publications is the book-publishing division
of TOUCH Outreach Ministries, a resource and consulting
ministry for churches with a vision for cell-based local
church structure.

Find us on the World Wide Web at
http://www.touchusa.org

To my wife CELYCE

My best friend and constant encouragement

CONTENTS

FOREWORD

Few things have affected the church worldwide as dramatically as cells. Throughout Europe, Asia, Africa, and North and South America, there is a hunger for teaching about how to develop cell-based churches. When the Lord began to speak to me about transitioning Bethany into a cell church, I read extensively about cell models and then took my pastoral staff to successful churches around the world to study the cell models on site. In each place, we saw churches bursting at the seams with life and the joy of the Lord. Thousands upon thousands of people were being saved and carefully integrated into well-defined cell churches. What I saw confirmed what God was saying to me — prepare for the coming harvest.

Perhaps that is why the title of Dr. Comiskey's book is intriguing to me: *Reap the Harvest*. I'm convinced that the Holy Spirit is speaking to the hearts of pastors and leaders around the world that a huge harvest of souls is coming and that we must be prepared. God is giving us the opportunity to ready our "nets" for the final ingathering of souls. For the last six years, Bethany has been re-tooling and is now a "full-fledged" cell church. Without apology, we eat, drink, and breathe "cells," and we are seeing the fruit of our efforts and the Holy Spirit's leading. Through cell relationships, we are reaching into homes, businesses, schools, and governments as never before.

The principles Dr. Comiskey identifies in this book are essential to a church transitioning to a cell-based church and to those who want to do cells better. His statement that there is a world of difference between a "church with cells" and a "cell church" is undeniably true. Because we don't want to get distracted, everything in our church is cell-related. When people are saved, immediately integrate them into a cell group. They don't know any different; so, to them, cells are what the church should be. We evangelize through cells, pastor through cells, and raise up and train leaders through cells.

If you are a pastor or church leader who is prayerfully considering a change to a cell-based church, you may be afraid that cells will alter the identity and uniqueness of your church. Bethany has always focused on prayer, missions, and evangelism. I can honestly say that, as a result of cells, we are praying with greater fervor, we are evangelizing in new and innovative ways, and we are on the verge of a tremendous missions harvest. Cells have only enhanced our identity. If you study the principles of the cell church and let the Holy Spirit guide you in the transition process, your church will become a stronger, healthier church with a renewed sense of its identity. Get ready to *Reap the Harvest* in the fields around your church!

Larry Stockstill
Senior Pastor, Bethany World Prayer Center

INTRODUCTION
CAN YOUR CHURCH GROW?

More people have become Christians in the last 10 years than in all of the church's previous history. Each DAY, 140,000 people are coming to the Lord! That is 46 times the number who believed on the day of Pentecost. In China, a country officially closed to the Gospel, more than 20,000 a DAY are turning to the Lord.[1] The number of evangelicals has doubled in just over 10 years, making this group the fastest growing movement or religion in the world.[2]

But is the church in North America keeping pace with the exciting growth that the rest of the world is experiencing? Clearly, the answer is that the church in North America has stagnated. Church attendance in the United States is at an all-time low.[3] More than 80 percent of the churches in the U.S. have plateaued or have declining Sunday morning attendance.[4] One-third of U.S. churches never grow beyond 50 members; two-thirds never grow beyond 150 members; and only 5 percent grow beyond 350 members.[5]

North America used to lead the world in exporting Christianity. Now we hear about amazing growth only in other parts of the world. What is the remedy for the ills confronting the North American church?

I believe that God wants us to reap the harvest once again in North America. Many churches today feel the need to return to small groups as modeled for us in the New Testament. They are choosing to concentrate on meeting the needs of their people through cell and celebration. Many of these small-group churches are experiencing phenomenal growth. Churches are seeing the potential and power of cell-based ministry.

Christian A. Schwarz, in his recent book, *Natural Church Development*, examined church-growth factors in over 1,000 churches in 32 countries. He concludes by saying, "If we were to identify any one principle as the 'most important,' then without a doubt it would be the multiplication of small groups."[6]

Cell churches are growing churches. This book will show you how to organize your church for growth around cell-group ministry. It will challenge you to rethink your church structure and prepare you to reach and receive a greater harvest.

YOU STARTED A SMALL-GROUP MINISTRY BUT ...

But what about the failures? Many churches have tried cell groups and failed. Many claim that small groups caused church splits, pastors to leave, and the proliferation of incorrect teaching. "I'm here to let you know that we don't believe in cell ministry. Small groups cause too many divisions." With this statement, a prominent board member successfully stamped out our pastoral initiative to become a cell-based church. This board member remembered the failure of starting a small-group ministry several years earlier: Leaders were found; five groups were started; and they were then left to die a slow, painful death. Such experiences have stirred opposition to cell-group ministry. Maybe your experience with small-group ministry has resulted in similar feelings. You are not alone.

Yet when you examine the churches that failed with small groups, the central problems have nothing to do with the cell group itself. Rather, the problems reside with the system behind the cell group. Therefore, this book is not about starting more small groups in your church. You've probably done that. And most likely you've seen them fade over the years.

The goal of this book is to help your church prepare for growth by developing a solid cell system. Why? So you can properly care for and feed your cells over the long haul. Strong cell systems produce effective cells. Churches that quickly launch cells often see them diminish over time. The difference lies in the system you develop, not in the cell model itself. This is why some cell churches succeed while others wither away.

SUCCESSFUL CELL-BASED CHURCHES

The largest churches in the world are structured to contain endless church growth. Their strategy places the cell group and the celebration at the center of their agenda. Cell churches care for their cells and also know how to gather the harvest into large celebration services.

You might be thinking, "But I know that celebration, congregation and cell are important. I've read about it for years." And yes, church-growth theorists have long written about the three C's. Yet, while acknowledging the importance of these three, churches still have started cells without establishing a strong cell system first. They've added cell groups without building the infrastructure common to all successful cell churches.

Many pastors and church leaders read about cell-group ministry and become hopeful for their church. They get excited about the prospect for success and begin to dream. So they start small groups.

But many fail to realize that they are erecting a house on the wrong foundation. The cell-group ministry was initiated without understanding what was necessary to make the cells work.

Some churches take another route. Before Bethany World Prayer Center transitioned to the cell system, the pastors were sent to the largest cell churches in the world. They took careful notes on the various cell systems they observed. With this information and a thorough knowledge of their own context, Bethany dug deeply and erected a cell infrastructure that models cell-church effectiveness to the rest of the world.

Perhaps you, like most people, are not able to visit the successful cell churches around the world. This book was written for you. I have been blessed with the opportunity to study them for you, and I believe the principles from these models can help you prepare your church to reap the harvest. These churches are located in eight different countries and four distinct cultures. They are:

Name of Church	Abbreviation	Country	Senior Pastor	No. of Cells	No. of Worshippers
Bethany World Prayer Center	BWPC	Baker, LA USA	Larry Stockstill	800	8,000
The Christian Center of Guayaquil	CCG	Guayaquil, Ecuador	Jerry Smith	2,000	7,000
Elim Church	EC	San Salvador, El Salvador	Mario Vega	6,000	35,000
Faith Community Baptist Church	FCBC	Singapore	Lawrence Khong	600	10,000
The International Charismatic Mission	ICM	Bogota, Colombia	César Castellanos	24,000	35,000[7]
Love Alive Church	LAC	Tegucigalpa, Honduras	René Peñalba	1,000	8,000
Living Water Church	LWC	Lima, Peru	Juan Captor	1,000	9,000
Yoido Full Gospel Church	YFGC	Seoul, Korea	David Cho	25,000	155,000[8]

I spent an average of eight days in each church. More than 700 cell leaders completed a questionnaire designed to discover why some leaders are able to multiply their groups and others are not.

The base of my study was expanded to include several churches using the Meta Model in the U.S., such as Willow Creek Community Church (South Barrington, Illinois), Saddleback Community Church (Saddleback, California), Cincinnati Vineyard (Cincinnati, Ohio), New Hope Community Church (Portland, Oregon), Fairhaven Alliance Church (Dayton, Ohio), and New Life Church (Colorado Springs, CO).

This book, then, investigates how and why churches built on a small-group foundation grow so rapidly and what we can learn and adapt from their systems. This book is for both pastors and lay leaders interested in fine-tuning their church for growth.

DESIGN YOUR CHURCH
FOR GROWTH

1

UNDERSTAND
CHURCH GROWTH

The phrase "church growth" stirs a negative reaction in many. Some say church-growth proponents have sold out to worldliness in order to "attract" visitors. "Come to my church and hear all about what I'm doing" is often the theme of the latest church-growth seminar.

Have you attended any of these seminars? I have. As a new pastor, I made my rounds to many of them, hoping that something would click. I listened, got excited, tried to apply the latest technique, and eventually dropped it when a newer church-growth method caught my interest.

At that point in my life, I had not articulated my philosophy of ministry. I did not view God as desiring to draw to Himself the men and women He created. In fact, it almost seemed like God wasn't interested in winning souls. My church was not growing as fast as I expected. I wanted people saved so I could be considered "successful;" so I twisted God's arm to produce numerical growth.

The allure of North American success and the latest church-growth teachings plummet many sincere, godly pastors into an inner struggle. Richard Halverson, former chaplain of the U.S. Senate, said: "When faith began in Palestine, it began with a relationship with a person, it moved to Greece and became a philosophy, it moved to Rome and became an institution, it moved to Europe and became a culture, it moved to the U.S. and became an enterprise."[1] He goes on to say, "The church is big business in the U.S. The entrepreneur is the pastor of the big church. ... Yet, 95 percent of the pastors are implicitly if not explicitly being told, 'Brother, if you're doing a good job, you'll be at the top.'"[2]

But let's not confuse the latest fad with the original principles of church growth delineated by Donald McGavran in his book *Understanding Church Growth*. Before reading this book, I was a fierce critic of church-growth philosophy. After pastoring a church for nearly five years, I wanted nothing to do with this movement. I even resisted taking a required course called "Church Growth." I entered into a heated argument with a colleague about the merits of church growth only a few days before the course began.

My professor, C. Peter Wagner, surprised me by openly discussing common criticisms of church growth, and he required each student to read a book positioned AGAINST it. Wagner also required us to read *Understanding Church Growth*, which helped me realize that church growth is not a method designed to "make me successful" as a pastor. Rather, it focuses on evangelizing the lost so they do not spend eternity in hell. McGavran's passion for evangelism permeates every page of that book.

As I weighed the pros and cons of church growth, I faced a decision. Would I accept McGavran's simple point about winning the lost and discipling them through Christ's church, or would I continue to reject this new philosophy? Despite the wide array of criticism against it, the church-growth philosophy compelled me to accept it.

I later discovered that the late Donald McGavran encouraged Ralph Neighbour Jr. to research the cell-church movement, visit David Yonggi Cho's church, and discover how cell ministry had revolutionized that church.

God Desires Your Church to Grow

God desires that His church grow both in quality and quantity. This sentence sums up the driving force of the church-growth movement. God's will is that none should perish. The apostle Peter wrote: "But do not forget this one thing, dear friends: With the Lord a day is like a thousand years, and a thousand years are like a day. The Lord is not slow in keeping His promise, as some understand slowness. He is patient with you, not wanting anyone to perish, but everyone to come to repentance" (2 Pet. 3:8-9). Paul wrote to his disciple Timothy: "This is good, and pleases God our Savior, who wants all men to be saved and to come to a knowledge of the truth. For there is one God and one mediator between God and men, the man Christ Jesus" (1 Tim. 2:3-5). God desires to save ALL men.

As a missionary to India, McGavran noticed that some churches grew rapidly while others in the same city became hopelessly stagnated. Instead of examining the reasons behind this discrepancy, many Christian leaders simply attributed the difference to the will of God. They believed that God willed some churches to grow and others to languish; therefore they concluded that God's people were called to faithfulness and not to question the mysteries of God.

But McGavran wasn't satisfied with such answers. He concluded from the Bible that God desires His church everywhere to grow in both quality and quantity. McGavran wrote, "Among other characteristics of mission, therefore, the chief and irreplaceable one must be this: that mission is a divine finding, vast and continuous. The chief and irreplaceable purpose of mission is church growth."[3]

Today, it's still all too common for pastors and leaders to relegate the growth rate of their churches to the "will of God." Many believe that if God desires numerical and qualitative growth, He will grant it. In other words, if there is no growth, it must be God's will. After all, leaders are called to faithfulness, not to success.

CHURCH GROWTH AND THE CELL CHURCH

I differ with those who diminish the importance of church growth in the cell-church movement, as if just knowing the methodology is sufficient. Although we can derive patterns and principles of cell ministry from the New Testament, if we're honest, we'll admit that the early church doesn't give us the one and only NT model of the church. Supporters of the House Church Movement, in fact, point to the same NT evidence to justify their model.

I find lots of NT evidence for the cell model, but, let's face it, the excitement for cell ministry today comes from the fact that it works. Churches are growing. I don't agree with those who tell you to "just hang in there" for long, long periods of time "even though you won't see growth for years." If your cell-church experiment doesn't provide dynamic church growth, you have every right to ask why! Right now. Don't base your excuse for the lack of growth on the New Testament church, because you won't find any consolation there. The growth rate of the NT church puts us to shame!

Why do people flock to the International Charismatic Mission in Bogota, Colombia? Is it simply because it's a cell church? Why do thousands of pastors attend the cell conferences at Bethany World Prayer Center? Is it simply because Bethany decided to do cell ministry? No, they go because it works. Cell-church ministry is capturing and holding the imagination of pastors because it works.

If your church is not growing, regardless of whether or not it has cells, you need to ask some tough questions. God designed His church for growth, and if growth is not taking place, then the keys to unlocking it will be found in this book.

You might insist, "I practice the cell church because it's THE biblical model." I congratulate you, and I agree that the cell model is biblically based. But you shouldn't practice cell ministry ONLY because of the biblical precedence. Practical concerns must fill your soul. Do you have a wide-open back door in your church?[4] Nothing will close it like cell ministry. Has your evangelism program lost steam? Cell ministry will give you new life. What about your pastoral care? Are you trying to do it on your own? The cell church offers a pastoral-care structure second to none.

GROW BOTH IN QUALITY AND QUANTITY

What kind of growth does God will? The "quality vs. quantity" debate has raged through the church for years. "I'm more concerned with quality than quantity," some say. "I don't play the numbers game," others assert. These arguments have their merits, because God is interested in the minute details of our lives, the very hairs on our head. Filling out statistical charts while overlooking the personhood of individuals is wrong.

But we must also be concerned for the multitude. Christ's ministry on this earth was a flurry of visits to villages, towns and cities. We read in Matthew 9:35-37 that,

> Jesus went through all the towns and villages, teaching in their synagogues, preaching the Good News of the kingdom and healing every disease and sickness. When he saw the crowds,

he had compassion on them, because they were harassed and helpless, like sheep without a shepherd. Then he said to his disciples, "The harvest is plentiful but the workers are few. Ask the Lord of the harvest, therefore, to send out workers into his harvest field."

Jesus constantly told His disciples that He must labor in other villages and in other places. After giving of Himself unreservedly, He found compassion for the multitudes who were as sheep without a shepherd. The answer is clear. Our churches need both quality and quantity. The book of Acts teaches us the need for both.

NUMERICAL GROWTH IN THE BOOK OF ACTS	SPIRITUAL GROWTH IN THE BOOK OF ACTS
1:15 — 120 were meeting 2:41 — 3,000 were added 4:4 — 5,000 men were added 5:14 — A great number were added 6:1 — The number of disciples was increasing 6:7 — The disciples increased rapidly 8:5-24 — Revival in Samaria 9:32-42 — Those living in Lydda and Sharon were converted 11:21-26 — A great number of people turned to the Lord in Antioch 13:43,44 — Many followed Paul 14:20,21 — A large number of disciples 16:5 — Galatia—churches grew in number daily 17:4 — Large number 17:12 — Many believed	1:14 — They all joined together 2:1-4 — They were filled with the Holy Spirit 2:42 — They continued in the apostle's doctrine 2:46 — They continued to meet together in the temple courts 4:24 — They lifted up their voice in one accord 4:32 — All the believers were in one heart and mind 12:24 — The Word of the Lord continued to increase and spread 13:49 — The Word of the Lord spread throughout the entire region 13:52 — The disciples were filled with joy and the Holy Spirit 16:5 — The churches were strengthened in the faith 17:11 — They examined the Scriptures every day 19:20 — The Word of the Lord spread widely and grew in power

"Is this 'cell church' concept simply a tool for church growth?" a recent visitor to my church asked. At first I didn't have an answer, but then I realized that he was wondering whether we were using cells strictly as a tool for quantitative growth. I assured him that cell-church ministry helped us grow continually in numbers while maintaining quality. Before fully implementing the cell system, we gathered a building full of Sunday worshippers but had little to offer them during the week. That changed when we introduced the cell-church system.

Churches are increasingly cognizant that they don't have to sacrifice quality for quantity. Healthy cell churches are growing churches. It's part of their genetic make-up. Yet, the built-in closeness of cells breathes New Testament life and ministry into these churches. Cells are small groups, rarely more than 12 people, and everyone feels important in this atmosphere. Personal care and ministry flourishes in this setting.

I was brought up in a church well known for its excellent youth and children's ministries. The church drew many adults (parents) and grew numerically because of these programs for children. Yet, because of the lack of adult ministry opportunities, most adults attended only the Sunday morning service. The youth pastor once commented that the Sunday morning numerical growth was superficial because adults could not experience the full meaning of "church" without contact with each other during the week.

I've wrestled with these questions: If someone attends only the Sunday morning worship service, has that person experienced the church of Jesus Christ? Is it possible just to sit passively, shake a few hands, sing a few songs, and consider that participation in the church? Isn't the true church of Jesus a living organism? Doesn't it demand interaction and participation? If someone does not experience fellowship and community in the church, has that person experienced the heartbeat of Christianity?

Those who attend an evangelical church normally receive a biblically sound and relevant message. This is good and right, and each person is given the chance to leave with new, applicable insight. Still, if a church member receives correct theological teaching without the very life of God pulsating from within, a serious imbalance results.

Most pastors determine who is "in their church" by Sunday worship attendance. For the most part, this is the accepted standard for determining whether a church is growing numerically. God wants His church to grow. I, too, desire to see as many new faces as possible on Sunday morning (primarily unchurched faces!). Like myself, most pastors diligently labor to fill their Sunday worship services as a sign that their church is growing, and that they are doing God's will.

Yet, if a church is content with the Sunday morning worship attendance as the key sign of success, is that church fulfilling the call of Jesus Christ? Could a church that is a model of "church-growth success" be rebuked by the Lord, "I know your deeds; you have a reputation of being alive, but you are dead" (Rev. 3:1)? Could it be that many do not know how to provide Christian community to their members? Perhaps there is a lack of knowledge concerning how to lead the congregation to a deeper sense of Christian fellowship. C. Kirk Hadaway touches this raw nerve by saying,

> However, as churches have grown larger and larger in the wake of rapid Christian advancement in recent times, churches, like society itself, have become more and more impersonal. They have come to reflect, understandably, the bureaucratic model, which increasingly has influenced all organizational forms in society, religious as well as secular. It is not enough to hear it from the pulpit, read it in the Bible, or see it in individuals. It has to be experienced in community.[5]

Cells are not just a church-growth technique; they are the key vehicle for the church of Jesus Christ to experience the true church in a living, dynamic way. The cell model depends on the success of both cell and celebration. One without the other doesn't suffice. Remember, we're talking about the cell church, not the CELL church or the cell CHURCH. We're promoting the CELL CHURCH. Celebration and cell make the motor work.

GOD HAS CHOSEN YOUR CHURCH TO REAP THE HARVEST

The church is the means by which God disciples a lost world. Unless a convert becomes a responsible member of a local church, evangelism is not complete. It's not enough to sow the seed. What pleases God most is harvesting. How does one know when there's a harvest? When the "seed sowing" and the decisions to follow Jesus as Lord and Savior result in increased church membership. Church-growth proponents teach that proclaiming the Gospel is not sufficient, that we must not be content until those people who receive Christ are gathered in His church. Church growth, plain and simple, is winning the lost and gathering them into the local church for the purpose of discipleship. Peter Wagner writes,

> How, then, is a disciple to be recognized? Obviously, it is a person who has turned from an old way of life and acknowledged Jesus as Lord and Savior. But just a verbal affirmation of faith is not enough. ... There are many fruits that are borne in the life of a true Christian through the Holy Spirit. However, the fruit that the Church Growth Movement has selected as the validating criterion for discipleship is responsible church membership.[6]

The cell church believes that responsible church membership requires participation both in Sunday celebration and weekly cell. While some cell churches I studied number into the hundreds of thousands of members, the membership does not feel lost. These gigantic churches are made up of thousands of small groups of five to 15 people who meet weekly for worship, ministry, outreach and fellowship.

GATHER THE HARVEST IN LIKE-MINDED GROUPS

When Donald McGavran made his famous statement, "Men like to become Christians without crossing racial, linguistic, or class barriers," a flood of criticism followed.[7] McGavran taught that evangelism is more effective among people of the same race, language and class. This is the "homogeneous unit" principle within church-growth thought. Thomas Rainer writes,

> When Donald McGavran began to advocate that principle as
> a tenet of church growth, an avalanche of criticism and debate
> ensued. Cries of 'racism,' 'narrow-mindedness,' 'exclusiveness,'
> and 'psychological manipulation' were voiced as a reaction to
> the much-debated principle.[8]

A homogeneous unit is a sufficiently large sociological grouping of individuals who perceive they have a common affinity for one another. One only has to look at the cultural landscape to see the vast grouping of like cultures in our world today. People of similar cultures naturally draw together, so why is there so much conflict in this area? Partly because many believe that church-growth advocates are promoting a subtle type of racism or that they're watering down the Gospel. However, the very heart of this principle is summed up by Rainer,

First, rapid evangelization takes place best when people of a culture share their faith in Jesus Christ with others within their own culture. Second, Christians must not insist that a person abandon his or her culture in order to become a Christian. Such is the essence of the homogeneous unit principle.[9]

Therefore, the homogeneous unit can be a helpful evangelistic tool but is never the goal of the Christian life. Cell groups take full advantage of this principle. Cells evangelize best when they function as homogeneous units. Individual cells forge natural ties built upon friendship, gender, class, occupation, neighborhood, or age grouping.

My wife, Celyce, has proven this principle true. She has a special concern for young mothers. As a mother of three small girls, she understands the joys and difficulties of motherhood. The cells in our church were not attracting this group of women. God stirred my wife to start a home cell group for this homogeneous group. Getting the women to share is not a problem in this cell. If anything, the difficulty is making sure everyone has a chance to share. These young mothers feel comfortable with those who face similar concerns and struggles.

Within eight months, Celyce's one cell group multiplied to five groups. Celyce knew from the beginning that she needed to start new groups to maintain the small, intimate atmosphere while reaching more mothers for Christ. One of the main reasons for this group's success is the intense interest among the young mothers to invite their friends and family members who are in the same stage of life. Like attracts like.

Bethany World Prayer Center reaches entire communities for Jesus Christ through its homogeneous cell groups. This church has discovered that people are more willing to invite their non-Christian friends to a homogeneous group than to a mixed group, and that those same friends are more resolved to attend such a group. Bethany added 300 homogeneous cell groups in just 18 months. Cell groups of this type naturally grow faster and are soon ready to give birth to daughter groups.

Yet, cell churches are by no means exclusive churches. They welcome all of God's rich creation. The homogeneous cells that meet during the week come together for a weekly Sunday celebration. In these festive moments, those from every tribe, language, and people celebrate together. Celebration in a cell church echoes the apostle John's words, "And they sang a new song: You are worthy to take the scroll and to open its seals, because you were slain, and with your blood you purchased men for God from every tribe and language and people and nation. You have made them to be a kingdom and priests to serve our God, and they will reign on the earth" (Rev. 5:9,10).

INVESTIGATE GROWING CHURCHES

Study of the human body was strictly forbidden in the Middle Ages. "After all," the church reasoned, "our bodies are the temple of God and should be held in great mystery." The lack of scientific investigation of the human body allowed diseases and other infirmities to abound. But that changed during the Enlightenment, when doctors put away their religious inhibitions and scientifically studied the human body. The results, of course, were incredible advances in medicine and discovery of new treatments.

Similarly, some people react negatively to investigating the church of Christ. "The church is a great mystery," they say, "and must be left that way." In contrast, McGavran proposed that God wanted His children to examine the reasons for growth and non-growth. After determining those factors (based on scientifically founded research) and looking carefully at each individual context, principles could be transferred to help God's church worldwide. Much of church growth will remain a mystery, but we can benefit from those principles common to growing churches.

I've studied the fastest-growing cell churches in the world to unlock the secrets of their growth. These churches demonstrate that growing rapidly in number while maintaining intimacy among the members is possible, and that both quality and quantity are essential. God desires both. Also, the key to successful cell ministry is not held by one culture alone. The principles work in a wide variety of cultures. Christian Schwarz, after studying 1,000 churches in 32 countries, concludes: "Our research in growing and declining churches all over the world has shown that continuous multiplication of small groups is a universal church growth principle."[10] These principles apply to your church also.

2

LEARN FROM CHURCHES
THAT REAP THE HARVEST

For 14 years, I had a secret dream to visit Yoido Full Gospel Church, the largest church in the history of Christianity. When I heard Pastor David Cho speak at Fuller Theological Seminary in 1984, I sat in awe of his simple yet powerful presentation of cell-group ministry. I bought all of Cho's tapes and listened to them over and over, hoping that something would click. As the young, inexperienced pastor of a pioneer church plant, I desperately sought direction. Along with the tapes, I devoured Cho's book *Successful Home Cell Groups* and taught cell principles to my leaders. But that didn't fulfill the dream. I still wanted to visit Yoido Full Gospel Church. God saw my private longing and fulfilled my desire in 1997.

YOIDO FULL GOSPEL CHURCH

As I strolled along the Han River and looked at the towering structure of Yoido Full Gospel Church, I praised God for the vision He placed

in this one man. YFGC sprang from the dreams and vision that God
gave David Yonggi Cho. He lives in a world of visions and dreams,
and he personally has lifted me to a higher understanding of vision
and leadership. His flaming vision has been passed on to thousands of
leaders. Cho writes,

> Everything starts from visions and dreams. Before you worry
> about giving birth to a child you must first become
> pregnant. So as a cell leader, you must become pregnant
> about your cell system and about soul winning. … So a clear
> goal and goal-led visions and dreams are very, very
> important. When people do not have visions, they do not
> believe. They do not work.[1]

God has blessed Cho's vision and dreams. More than 150,000
people attend the mother church each Sunday, with 100,000 more in
the ten satellite churches around Seoul. The 25,000 cell groups pastor
each member. Without the cell system, this church could not grow so
rapidly and continually. Apart from the cell system, there is no way a
church could care for such a great number of believers.

YFGC initiated the modern cell-church movement.[2] God brought
Cho to a place of surrendering his own initiatives and plans in favor
of God's. In his hour of trial, Cho reread the New Testament through
the eyes of early house churches. He saw that the first-century
Christians meeting in homes actually practiced the priesthood of all
believers. Cho handed his ministry over to laypeople, and the world
has stood in awe ever since.

Cho depends on the cell system to spiritually feed each member.
YFGC's 1997 annual church-growth conference brochure says, "The
home cell has been the backbone of Yoido Full Gospel Church. Any
church that wishes to implement this concept has to be completely

reorganized into a cell-based church."[3]

Approximately 24 districts, organized geographically, serve as the nerve centers for the church. Each district has paid staff who are available to counsel, encourage or just be a friend to those in their district. When I visited on Sunday, these offices were a beehive of activity as staff pastors ministered to their people.[4]

Each district has 12 to 23 sub-districts, and each sub-district contains 10 to 15 sections. Each section contains five to 15 home cell groups. Each cell has approximately five to 10 households.

When we think of aggressive evangelism and church growth in Korea, we usually think of Pastor Cho's church. However, nine other churches in Korea have more than 30,000 members. Without exception, they have experienced rapid growth by structuring their church around cell-group ministry.

BETHANY WORLD PRAYER CENTER

Bethany World Prayer Center is on the cutting edge in North America and destroys the myth that cells will not work in the U.S.! Since establishing cells as the base of the church in 1993, BWPC has experienced record growth year after year. In the last four years, BWPC has registered over 5,000 conversions through cell groups alone (not including conversions in worship services, etc.).[5] Some 1,200 pastors flock to Bethany's cell seminars held every eight months. Bethany is proving to the North American church that cell-church ministry is both relevant and effective.

That wasn't always the case. BWPC did not grow from 1990 to 1992. The church was winning souls and the leadership thought it was growing. However, while many were entering the church, an equal number were leaving at the same time. Under the direction of Senior Pastor Larry Stockstill, Bethany began its transition to a cell church with 54 cells. The cell ministry successfully closed the back door of the church. In fact, 600 families were added to the church that same year.[6] By the end of 1998, Bethany had more than 800 weekly cells and a church family of over 8,000 people.

Bethany World Prayer Center is God's gift to the world. It gives about $2 million annually to missions. The church is debt-free, and its mission's budget automatically increases by $100,000 every year.

FAITH COMMUNITY BAPTIST CHURCH

Faith Community Baptist Church mushroomed from 600 members in 1986 to the present 10,000 as a result of a home cell-group explosion. This church exemplifies the power of both cell and celebration.

During my visit to Singapore, the whole church gathered in a rented indoor stadium for a celebration service. About 40 worship team members took to the stadium floor. Dancers in bright, colorful costumes swayed and danced to the music. The worship leaders alternated between Chinese and English as they exhorted the congregation to enter into the presence of Jesus Christ.

The organization of FCBC combines Ralph Neighbour Jr.'s years of experience with Lawrence Khong's strong leadership. Its cell system is a pacesetter in the world today; It's probably the most organized cell church I have witnessed. More than 120 pastoral staff and 77 administrative staff care for the 600 cell groups.

Cells work at FCBC because of the cell system behind them. The system is organized for growth, and the church is seeing the results. FCBC has combined the efficiency of the geographical district with the need for specialized ministry better than any other cell church. At FCBC you will find both homogeneous cell groups (Campus District, Youth Zone, Music Zone, Chinese District, Handicap District) as well as geographical cell groups (three large districts). This system maximizes the growth potential by offering people a choice. You can join a particular type of cell (homogeneous groups) or simply attend the cell nearest your house (geographical districts).

THE INTERNATIONAL CHARISMATIC MISSION

After struggling as a pastor for nine years, in 1983 César Castellanos was about to give up. At that point, the Lord intervened with a vision that changed his life. The Lord told Pastor Castellanos that his converts would number more than the stars of the sky and the sand by the seashore.

The first step toward realizing this vision was for Castellanos to dream about it, even to the point of hearing car doors close and feet shuffling as he envisioned 200 people who would be added to his congregation. In the three months that followed, his church skyrocketed from eight members to 200. In 1990, ICM had seventy cell groups; in 1994, about 1,200. ICM exploded between 1995 and 1997. In 1996 alone, the number of cells grew from 4,000 to 10,500. By June 1998, there were 24,000 cell groups. The goal for 2000 AD is 50,000 cell groups and 500,000 people attending Sunday worship.

The church, one of the fastest growing in the world, has expanded so rapidly that it now gathers in a stadium in Bogota, Colombia. About 17,000 young people meet every Saturday night in the indoor stadium. On Sunday morning, the church has three services. The 24,000 cell groups minister to this huge congregation. ICM is showing the rest of the world how to transform cell members into cell leaders. The leadership training cycle is so powerful that non-Christians are often saved, turned around, and leading their own cell within six months.

The International Charismatic Mission encourages each member to disciple twelve people — just like Jesus. Each cell leader constantly searches for potential cell leaders among the cell members. When a cell member finishes the required training and starts to lead his own cell group, he becomes a disciple of the parent cell leader. Thus the cells are constantly multiplying.

The key to position within this church is the fruit. They follow Jesus' teaching: "This is to my Father's glory, that you bear much fruit, showing yourselves to be my disciples" (John 15:8). Little or no fruit means no place in leadership. Advancement in leadership depends almost completely upon whether a cell leader multiplies groups. To even be considered for a pastoral staff position, a member must multiply to 250 cell groups!

Disciples whose lives lack fruit are given time to mend their ways and reconcile with God. They are asked to step down if no improvement occurs, and a "Timothy" or an assistant leader takes his or her place. This flexible and varied structure gives every member both responsibility and the opportunity to serve.

ELIM CHURCH

"We couldn't leave our house for three weeks. Bullets were flying everywhere," said one cell leader. "Did you continue to meet as a cell group?" I inquired. "Of course," the cell leader replied. "We're also soldiers in a spiritual warfare." The testimony of this cell leader was hardly unique to Elim Church in San Salvador.

The civil war that raged through El Salvador from 1981 to 1992 claimed 75,000 lives. But through the blood-stained tears, the evangelical church grew from 2.3 percent of the population to over 20 percent. The growth at Elim Church has been so tremendous that the cell groups rent over 600 city buses to carry cell members to the celebration services. Cell leaders, like warriors of light, minister around the clock and bring bright hope to an otherwise troubled land.

Pastor Solórzano visited Cho's church in Korea in 1986. He returned convinced that cell-group ministry would revolutionize Elim Church. By 1991, six years later, cell-group attendance had grown to 57,000 with a large proportion attending the Sunday celebration services.[7] Today over 130,000 people participate in the 6,000 cell groups, and about 35,000 worship together on Sunday mornings.

This church believes that the harvest is plentiful. The cell groups have penetrated the entire city for Jesus Christ. Over 130,000 people attend cell groups that span the entire city. While visiting this church, I asked strangers about Elim and every one knew about it and could describe it, even though I was more than thirty minutes away from the church building. Even in the midst of a raging war, the cells at Elim Church dispelled the darkness with the Good News of the Gospel.

Elim Church is perhaps the most recognized cell church in Latin America. The cell group system at EC is the key to the church's success. Hundreds of people flock to this church each year to learn about its powerful cell ministry. Many churches are following the EC model and have large, dynamic cell churches.[8]

Although Latin Americans are frequently portrayed as lacking organizational abilities, this is certainly not true of EC.[9] Statistics, graphics and percentages help the members determine exactly where they stand at any given moment. Goals are made and tracked on every level. Through the organization of the cell system, every person receives personal contact. Each district coordinator, zone pastor, supervisor and cell leader knows exactly what to do to make the system work effectively.

CONCLUSION

Many other model cell churches could have been included in this chapter. For example, Dion Robert's Baptist church in the Ivory Coast has grown to 120,000 members in 8,000 cell groups since organizing as a cell church in 1983 (with some 683 members).[10] While cells form the basis for its organization, Pastor Robert has developed a system that specifically works for the unique situation in West Africa.

Your church is unique. It isn't Faith Community Baptist Church or Elim Church. God has something special for your church in your context. You can, however, glean principles from these model cell churches. You can learn which systems are needed to contain the growth that God wants to give you. As you understand their systems, you will increase your ability to develop the kind of church God wants to build in your city. These system principles will help you build a firm foundation in order to hold a greater harvest.

3

BUILD A STRONG
CELL SYSTEM

The successful cell systems located throughout the world are divergent, yet they share common principles. Each of these churches has adopted key principles fundamental to developing a strong cell system. Then they adapted them to its particular circumstances. These strong, healthy cell systems in turn make powerful cell churches. What are these common principles?

1. Dependence on Jesus Christ Through Prayer

Jesus Christ, the head of the church, is the only One who can grant success. These churches depend on Jesus to answer their prayers. Prayer is not just talked about but consistently practiced by these Christians. Each church holds regular all-night prayer meetings. The two largest churches do so weekly. One cell church gathers for fasting and prayer on national holidays. These churches practice total dependence on God. For example, several people at the International

Charismatic Mission said, "Copying our system without the power of the Spirit of God through prayer is like buying a car without a motor." North Americans tend to become enamored with the model, the system. But the system without power from the One who makes it run will produce little fruit.

2. Motivation for Cell Ministry is Evangelism and Church Growth

Some people believe that the main purpose of cell ministry is edification of the saints, or even pastoral care. But the largest cell churches in the world tell a different story. These churches strategically planned to conquer their cities for Christ, and their cell ministry made this feat possible.

Pro-active evangelism characterizes these churches, and cell ministry enabled them to maintain momentum and bypass stagnation as they crossed growth barriers. Cho writes: "There is only one way that the home cell group system will be successful in a church, if that system is to be used as a tool of evangelism."[1]

3. Multiplication: The Goal of Each Cell Group

Although different in their method of multiplication, all of these churches are primarily concerned about cell-group evangelism that results in cell multiplication. This is the clear and stated focus of the cell ministry in each church. The cell vision is outward focused. Group fellowship is always present but is more of a by-product than a goal. Static, non-growing cell groups are simply unacceptable. In each church, the new cell leaders immediately know their mission: cell reproduction.

Reaching out to unbelievers and penetrating the neighborhood with the Gospel of Jesus Christ is the rallying cry of each cell group. Cell groups are to be salt and light in a dark, desperate world. Of course, there is a danger for cells to become cozy clubs for the initiated, but this must be avoided at all costs. God calls cell groups to evangelize, grow and multiply. After Christian Schwarz analyzed the 4.2 million responses in his worldwide church-growth study, he writes: "We asked all survey participants … about concrete [multiplication] plans for their own group. Virtually no other aspect of church life has such an enormous influence on both the quality index and the growth of a church."[2]

Cells in the churches I studied were expected to multiply over and over, utilizing the ever-expanding web of members' relationships. 60 percent of the 700 cell leaders who answered my questionnaire had multiplied their group at least once. Again, passion for the lost is the motivation that keeps everything in perspective. As the cells continue to expand and multiply, the leadership base extends to a wide cross-section of culture. Rapid growth is maintained, new leaders emerge, close fellowship takes place, and the church grows as a result.

4. Designed for Reproducible Quality Control

Cells reproduce more easily when "quality control" is maintained through the cell system. Quality control means that all cell groups maintain similar components or characteristics. All of the cell groups, for example, meet regularly for the purpose of spiritual edification and evangelistic outreach (with the goal of multiplication) and are committed to participate in the functions of the local church. This is the working definition of all the small groups studied. It isn't enough to be "small" and a "group" to be called a cell group. No, all cell groups in these churches maintain similar components: spiritual growth, evangelistic outreach (with the goal of multiplication), and an intimate connection with the local church.

Billy Hornsby, national director of Bethany Cell Church Network, tells the story of a nearby restaurant that cooked excellent food but still went out of business. The chefs were experts at what they were doing, but having that expertise wasn't enough. Why? Because right across the street McDonald's was training high-schoolers in six weeks to make better hamburgers than the great restaurant. McDonald's chose to perfect a few products and then distribute them widely in order to maintain quality control.[3] Similarly, Bethany World Prayer Center has developed a reproducible cell ministry by multiplying the same type of cell group. Each cell, in other words, features the same components: knowing God, knowing each other, and reaching the world for Christ. Cells multiply again and again because the same genetic make-up or "quality control" is transferred from cell to cell.

5. Emphasis on Goal-Setting

In the human body, each biological cell grows and reproduces its parts until it divides into two cells. Those two cells in turn divide and reproduce themselves. In the same way, the goal of each cell in these churches is always evangelism that results in multiplication.

Since cell multiplication is a way of life, the churches are unashamed to set clear goals. There is no hidden agenda or attempt to mince words. The major quantitative goal is the number of new cell groups to be formed.[4] The International Charismatic Mission and The Christian Center of Guayaquil display the year-end goal for new cell groups on highly visible banners hanging from the front wall of the church. Everyone entering the building is immediately reminded of the church's specific goal and of its completion date.

Pastor César Castellanos, a man of action, will not rest until the church goal is reached. He says, "All of the growth that we've obtained thus far has come by focusing on specific goals. When I began my ministry, God said to me, 'What do you want and when do you want it.'"[5] This is a common trait of the leaders within each of these churches.

6. Cell Ministry Is the Church's Backbone

The one phrase repeated over and over again in these churches is that cell ministry is the "backbone" of the church. The vision passed down from senior pastors to leaders to members is that a person must belong to a cell group in order to receive any type of pastoral care.

They are not just adding cell ministry as another program. Rather, cells are the very life of the church. These churches organize pastoral staff, specific programs, membership, baptisms, offerings, and celebration services around cell ministry. Everyone in the church is expected to attend a cell. One church revealed statistics showing that 90 percent of the 7,500 weekend worshippers also participate in a weekly cell group.[6]

7. Importance of Both Cell and Celebration

Some people presume that the cell is more important than the celebration service. Yet successful cell churches tell a different story. Celebration and cell attendance are two sides of the same coin: One is not sufficient without the other, and both are essential for success in the cell church. The meaning of the phrase "cell church" implies cell and celebration working as equal parts of the cell system. Members attend both cell and celebration as opposed to just one or the other.

These churches carefully link cell ministry to the celebration service. In other words, precaution is taken to guarantee that individual cells share the same vision and philosophy as the mother church. In each church, at least 65 percent of those who attend the celebration service also attend a cell group.

This point needs to be carefully emphasized because of the growing House Church Movement around the world. In this movement, each house church is independent or only loosely connected to other house churches. But listen to how David Cho, the father of the modern cell-church movement, intimately connects the cell with celebration: "The local church is the strength of Christianity. Home cell groups contribute to that strength. Anything that dilutes the strength of the local church is to be avoided."[7]

8. Senior Pastor's Strong, Visionary Leadership

Successful cell churches are led by strong senior pastors, because the cell system flows from the authority of the senior pastor. While visiting these churches, I detected a great respect and willingness to follow among the members. All of these senior pastors hold unchallenged authority.

Without exception these pastors are men of vision and dreams. Their ultimate church-growth goals encompass hundreds of thousands of people. They are out to conquer a city for Christ, not just grow a church. Two of the pastors openly talk about the importance of dreaming big dreams and use Cho as their example. Because of the pastoral vision, the members in turn sense that they are part of a work greater than themselves and that God Himself has spoken to their pastor.

The active leadership of the head pastor in the direction of the cell ministry is a clear, distinguishing mark in the cell church. Cho declares, "The pastor must be the key person involved. Without the pastor, the system will not hold together. It is a system, and a system must have a control point. The controlling factor in home cell groups is the pastor."[8]

In my research and experience in cell-based churches, I have discovered that the role of the senior pastor is crucial to the long-term success of the cell ministry. The direction of cell ministry cannot be delegated to someone else.

9. Established Leadership Requirements

All of the cell churches have clearly defined cell leadership and training requirements. Although these vary from church to church, the core requirements include salvation, water baptism, cell attendance and completion of cell training.

10. Required Leadership Training

Even if a potential cell leader meets the basic leadership requirements, he needs to complete a leadership training process. The length and demands of the course vary widely among the churches.

All of these churches are compelled to find, train and release new leadership as quickly and efficiently as possible. For example, the declared goal of the International Charismatic Mission is to transform every new convert into a dynamic cell leader. Leadership training here includes a two-day spiritual retreat, two core leader training courses, and another spiritual retreat.

Most successful cell churches around the world provide:

1. Pre-training for potential cell leaders before they begin leading groups.
2. An apprentice system within the cell group, through which potential leaders are trained from the moment they enter the group.
3. A Jethro system in which every leader is pastored.[9]
4. On-going training (weekly, bimonthly or monthly).

11. Leadership Developed Within the Church

These churches look no farther than themselves to fill top leadership positions.[10] They do not look to seminaries or Bible colleges for their leaders. Without exception, all leadership goes through the normal channels of ministerial experience, ministerial success, and leadership training within the church before being given higher levels of responsibility.

12. A "Jethro Model" Care Structure

These churches would not have grown so large had it not been for the intimate care for each leader. All of these churches rely on a pastoral leadership plan to care for everyone in cell leadership. Each leader is monitored, pastored, and made accountable. The burden on the head pastor in traditional churches is relieved in the cell church through a hierarchical structure of leadership that cares for groups of thousands, hundreds, fifties and tens. The philosophy behind this model is Jethro's advice to Moses in Exodus 18 about how to delegate leadership responsibilities. Some cell churches set leaders over geographical districts, zones and areas of the city. Others supervise their leaders through homogeneous departments. The fundamental leadership role, however, is always given to the cell leader.

13. Leadership Promotion Based on Success

Elevation in ministry to higher positions of leadership is primarily a result of previous success in cell multiplication. Although calling and personal qualities are taken into account, the ultimate test is past success as a cell leader. Even Bible school training is not a major factor in elevation to top leadership.

14. Cell Groups Meet in Homes

All of these churches use the home as the primary meeting place for the cell groups. On the other hand, training takes place in the temple. The church building is utilized to its maximum potential in order to prepare leadership to minister in the home.[11]

15. Cells Follow-up with Visitors, New Converts

In all of these churches, the cells disciple the visitors and new converts. New visitor cards are collected in the churchwide celebration service. These cards are distributed to the various cell groups, which in turn disciple the newcomers. These churches provide an organizational system to check whether each new person is attending the cell group.

At Bethany World Prayer Center, for example, a cell leader stands behind the person at the altar during one of the regular invitations. Following the altar ministry, the new believer is led upstairs to the district offices and warmly greeted. The person then is directed to one of the seven district offices based upon his ZIP code. The new believer views a video of Bethany, is introduced to cell life, and then meets his appropriate zone pastor. Within 24 hours a staff pastor and cell leader visit the new believer at home![12]

16. Cell Lessons Based on Pastor's Sermon

To assure continuity between the cells and the celebration service, the cell lessons in each church are based on the senior pastor's preaching. Although each church uses a different style or format for creating the lesson, without exception, the pastor's message is the foundation.

For example, at the Living Water Church in Lima, Peru, a talented leader takes diligent notes of the pastor's message in order to weave his thoughts into the weekly cell lesson. At the Christian Center in Guayaquil, Ecuador, the senior pastor personally prepares the weekly cell lesson. Although each church uses a different method, the senior pastor's message is the launching point for the cell group topic. The lesson might be a summary of the Sunday message or four carefully designed application questions that follow the Sunday morning message.[13]

CONCLUSION

Bethany World Prayer Center has grown to over 8,000 people in 800 cells. International Charismatic Mission now has 24,000 groups. The largest church in history, Yoido Full Gospel Church, has over 155,000 people attending worship every week. This kind of growth did not happen overnight nor did it transpire magically. Much prayer and thought has gone into the development of these churches. They did not put people into small groups and tell them to meet every week. The cells in these churches work because they have systems in place to support the groups and their leaders. System components found in all these churches make the cells work. The rest of this book expands on these components. For more instruction on

- Motivation for Cell Ministry is Evangelism and Church Growth, see **Chapters 1, 2 & 5**
- Multiplication: The Goal of Each Cell Group, see **Chapters 1, 2 & 5**
- Dependence on Jesus Christ Through Prayer, see **Chapter 4**
- Designed for Reproducible Quality Control, see **Chapter 5**
- Emphasis on Goal-Setting, see **Chapters 1, 2 & 5**
- Cell Ministry Is Church's Backbone, see **Chapter 8**
- Senior Pastor's Strong, Visionary Leadership, see **Chapter 9**
- A "Jethro Model" Care Structure, see **Chapter 10**
- Established Leadership Requirements, see **Chapter 11**
- Required Leadership Training, see **Chapter 11**
- Leadership Developed Within Church, see **Chapter 11**
- Leadership Promotion Based on Success, see **Chapter 11**
- Cells Follow-up with Visitors and New Converts, see **Chapters 6 & 12**
- Importance of Both Cell and Celebration, see **Chapter 13**
- Cell Lessons Based on Pastor's Sermon, see **Chapter 13**

The above principles should serve as a checklist as you develop your small-group system. Remember that the growing cell churches around the world excel in these areas. Study each principle along with the corresponding chapter(s), and then rate your own cell system.

Some chapters will provide more immediate help than others, depending on your situation. Perhaps you are particularly weak in establishing small groups as the "backbone" of your church. You will need to master the message embodied in Chapter 8. Or maybe your celebration service needs fine-tuning. Concentrate on Chapter 13. All of these principles are essential, but it will take time to perfect all of them. As you hone your small-group system based on these principles, Jesus Christ will use your church in a fresh, dynamic way.

BASE YOUR CHURCH
UPON SPIRITUAL DYNAMICS

4

DEPEND

ON THE SPIRIT

A pastor invited me to attend a cell seminar that he hoped would bring new life to his dying church. As I attended the seminar with him and visited his church, I witnessed the pastor's enormous struggle to survive. The church was on its last breath. Only a handful of the faithful continued the arduous journey year after year. They hung on despite multiple changes in pastors, deep-rooted tradition and declining membership. My friend wouldn't quit without a fight; he possessed too much pride. He devoured every new book on church growth and tested each new strategy, with practically no success. He was grasping at straws, and the latest one was cell groups. "Could this seminar save a nearly hopeless situation?" he wondered.

I believe in cell seminars and conduct many each year. But even if God leads a pastor to implement the cell system in his church, a cell seminar alone won't cure the ills of a dying body. Only Jesus the

Great Physician — not small groups — can heal a stagnated church. "We must never forget that small groups are not the answer. ... Jesus is the answer to our problems. We need to be careful not to deify the form of small groups," says Michael Mack, founder of The Small Group Network.[1] I love small-group ministry and fervently believe the church desperately needs it. But only Jesus can grant new life and dynamic growth.

THE POWER BEHIND THE CELL CHURCH

"My people follow me because they see the power of God in my life," said Luis Salas, a member of Castellanos' pastoral team at ICM. "They notice how God answers my prayers, and they believe that He will do the same for them." Salas has launched hundreds of cell groups in the past two years, and he gives all the glory to the active presence of Jesus Christ in his life. Successful cell churches expect God to move and to perform miracles today just as He did in the first-century church.

Cell churches contain the power, the current of the Holy Spirit. They don't automatically produce that current. If your church is choking the life of the Spirit of God, don't expect cells to remedy your problem. You must first invite God to fix the basic problem and clean the rusty pipes that impede His flow. He uses the cell system, but He winces at being used by it.

Cell-church organization enhances the life of the Spirit and allows the Spirit to flow more freely than a traditional church structure. But if forced to choose between cell structure or the Spirit of God, I wouldn't hesitate to invite the Holy Spirit on my team.

Many pastors think that a church with people in groups is a cell church. "Get more people in small groups and the church will grow" is their philosophy. But this attitude misses the point. Cell churches do not thrive without the flow of the Holy Spirit. Churches may successfully transition to a cell system, but without the Spirit of God they end up as empty wineskins without the new wine. Cells won't make your church grow. Only the Spirit of God moving through people in community will resurrect a dead church.

Pastors from around the world are flocking to The International Charismatic Mission, the world's fastest-growing cell church. Some pastors visit ICM and copy everything about the church, even changing their names to include the word "charismatic." These pastors buy the same kind of seats used at ICM; they start multiple services like ICM; but their churches don't grow.

One pastor visiting ICM asked me, "Do you know how to become a millionaire?" "No," I replied. "Copy everything that a millionaire does," he responded. This pastor journeyed to Bogota intent on replicating every ICM program, schedule and activity in his own church of 80 members. He thought that these changes would turn his church into the next ICM. Sadly, such thinking greatly errs. This pastor didn't realize that copying the outward activity of a program or a person doesn't transfer the ingrained values. Those convictions are developed over a lifetime of testing, proving, and adapting.

You can learn and practice the precise methodology of ICM and fail miserably. Why? Along with the methodology, you need the revival of the church, the dependence on the Spirit of God, and the burden for prayer. Castellanos, the founder and senior pastor of ICM, wisely says,

> The secret is not in the method. How many times have we become in love with a certain method? ... But I want you to know that the actor on life's stage today is you. God has a new fresh anointing for you. He wants to release this anointing for you.[2]

His wife, Claudia Castellanos, voices the same concern about those who would blindly follow methods. She says, "Those who have the power of the Spirit of God have the power of creativity."[3]

Many Christian leaders lack this "power of creativity." It's easier to follow the creativity and trodden path of someone else. It requires less work. Each church's circumstances are unique. Only God knows the intimate details of your church, and He alone can create the "right fit." You will find that "right fit" as you depend on the Holy Spirit and seek His direction. Don't copy someone else's creativity. Allow the Spirit to give you fresh insight, then follow it each day.

DEPENDENCE ON THE SPIRIT THROUGH PRAYER

I'll admit that I didn't want to get out of bed. Our team planned to attend the 5 A.M. prayer meeting at the International Charismatic Mission, but I secretly hoped that my head pastor wouldn't hear the alarm clock. I was worn out from the previous day's activity. But Pastor Porfirio heard the alarm and alerted the rest of us. We stumbled out of bed and arrived at the church at 5:30. We sat through each consecutive prayer meeting: 5, 6, 7, 8 and 9 A.M. What did we learn? ICM succeeds because of the person of Jesus Christ. Christ gives the marching orders. He commands the troops. As His people submit to Him in prayer, He grants success. The counsel we heard over and over was, "You must first win the battle in prayer; success naturally follows."

Growing cell churches know how to pray. They realize that prayer moves God's hand and unleashes His power to work. They understand that nothing happens apart from His work. Take, for example, Bethany World Prayer Center. As its name suggests, Bethany World Prayer Center places prayer at the foundation of its existence. The cell ministry started by dividing the intercessory prayer warriors into cell groups. Prayer warriors led prayer warriors in those initial days. No wonder those first 50 cells multiplied to 108 cells in just six months! Prayer (along with fasting) sets Bethany apart as the premier cell church in the U.S. today.

Members of the largest church in history, Yoido Full Gospel Church, quickly credit secret prayer for their public success. Members wrestle in prayer. The imagery of soldier and warrior best portray the church members. What a thrill to walk by the grottos at Prayer Mountain and hear the cries and pleas of Korean saints ascending like incense to the throne of God! About 1,000 prayer warriors pass through Prayer Mountain every day. Many of these dear saints are dedicated to personal prayer as well as corporate prayer. One morning, I saw approximately 3,000 people pray fervently in the main auditorium — at five o'clock! Loud cries echoed throughout the auditorium as the believers prayed in unison. This is "a spiritual church."

How can you promote prayer in your church? First and most importantly, the senior pastor must lead the way. People will follow what the senior pastor models, not just what he says. If the senior pastor is a man of prayer, the people will be a church of prayer. Second, welcome a wide variety of prayer options in your church. If some are willing to gather at the church at 7 A.M., gladly receive them. Appoint a prayer warrior to lead them. If the afternoon is better for others, accommodate them. Remember that Christ promises to abide in the midst of two or three gathered in His name. Third, encourage your cell groups to pray. Include specific petitions on your cell lesson handout.

GOD IS CALLING HIS CHURCH TO REPENTANCE

Jesus was talking to the church when He said: "Here I am! I stand at the door and knock. If anyone hears my voice and opens the door, I will come in and eat with him, and he with me" (Rev. 3:20). Jesus longs to be an "insider" in our churches today. Sadly, He's standing outside of many. God showed César Castellanos that the North American church is like a man who bought his wife a beautiful home and all the best things to fill it. Then she became entertained with all the things and put her husband out of the house. "That is the condition of the American church," he heard the Lord say. "They have kept MY things, but they have pushed ME out, and I am on the outside."[4]

Repentance in the New Testament includes a turning from sin and turning to the Lord. It embodies the notion of changing one's mind and entering a new way of thinking. We need to turn from over-dependence on methods and realize that churches need Jesus Christ to produce true fruit. He counsels us to take from Him the "… gold refined in the fire so you can become rich; and white clothes to wear, so you can cover your shameful nakedness; and salve to put on your eyes, so you can see" (Rev. 3:18).

We must not place the cell model before the person of Jesus Christ. Nor should we promise our church something that only Jesus can offer. God is stirring His people to dedicate themselves to prayer and to trust in the Spirit of God. His life is imparted through constant communion, time spent in His presence. Pay the price in prayer, and your cell ministry will direct God's power to a lost and dying world.

5

REAP THE BENEFITS OF
THE CELL CHURCH

"Why should I change to the cell church paradigm? After all," you might say, "I know that the Holy Spirit must give victory and I'm praying more; why should I change my present church structure?" The questions "What's in it for me?" and "How can cell ministry make a positive difference in my church?" are valid and relevant. Here are a few reasons to take a serious, prayerful look at the cell church.

EVANGELISM THAT RESULTS IN BOTH SALVATION AND SANCTIFICATION

Evangelism programs. Take your pick from the dozens on the market today. I'm not knocking these programs. I have greatly benefited by learning how to share the Gospel in a succinct and understandable manner. Yet the trouble with evangelism programs is what comes afterward. Leading someone to Jesus is fairly simple; the difficulty lies in making that person a disciple of Jesus Christ. Many evangelism programs end when a person receives Christ. Then we have to begin another program called "follow-up."

I've prayed with hundreds of people to receive Jesus. But as the years passed, I could hardly contain the creeping doubt concerning the whereabouts of these people. As far as I knew, they weren't attending an evangelical church. "God knows what happened to them," I persistently told myself. Eventually, I became honest. "Souls in the belt" of a zealous evangelist often fall by the wayside.

The church doesn't need more information about how to lead others to Jesus Christ. Discipleship is the cry of the church today. The challenge is to convert the lost in such a way that we don't need another program of follow-up. Because of the dichotomy of salvation and sanctification, millions of undisciplined baby sheep roam the countryside. They've accepted Christ as their Savior but have not been discipled in His body.

Bethany World Prayer Center has employed nearly every gimmick to attract newcomers and lead them to Jesus Christ. They've promoted dogs jumping through hoops, Spirit-filled weight lifters, and other stunts to attract people and grow the church. Through such events, thousands upon thousands of unbelievers have received Christ. But these programs couldn't hold the harvest.[1] Bethany has learned the hard way, through experience, that evangelism is best accomplished through relationships in small groups rather than through big events.

The atmosphere in a small group is safe for non-Christians, especially if the group meets in a home. Group time begins with food and an icebreaker. "What was the first car you remember riding in?" or "What was the first trophy you received?" are examples of friendly icebreakers. Afterward, the facilitator introduces the theme of the lesson — say, loneliness. By this point, the non-Christian is caught in the web of personal evangelism. After someone receives Christ (more than 80 to 100 people receive Jesus at Bethany every month), the cell provides natural, built-in follow-up.[2]

"I feel confused," Dora, a non-Christian, confessed one night. The members of my cell didn't pounce on her to repeat a prayer. We encouraged her and prayed for her. Six weeks later, Dora prayed the "sinner's prayer" with my wife, Celyce, in our home. Because she was already a faithful cell member, we had built-in follow-up. I had the privilege of baptizing Dora in our church. What a difference it makes when someone receives Christ in a small group!

Salvation is instantaneous. The sanctification process takes time. One of the primary reasons small-group churches are growing so rapidly is because salvation and sanctification naturally occur within the cell. But it doesn't stop there.

As new Christians develop in Christ's likeness, cell members encourage them to attend the celebration service as well. New converts are exposed to the preaching of the Word and the sacraments, and see that they are essential for spiritual growth. Cell leaders and members know their work isn't complete until the convert becomes a responsible church member. Cell workers also recognize, however, that identification with the mother church can take time. New converts initially feel more comfortable with their friends in the small group.

NEW MEMBERS HAVE A
PLACE TO BELONG

During my first ministry in Ecuador, I served on the pastoral team in a middle-upper class church called El Batán. We tried to close the back door of the church by pastoring new converts more effectively. At the time, about 550 people attended the church. Ten weeklong evangelistic campaigns each year brought us a constant flow of visitors, many of whom dedicated their lives to Jesus. Yet we continually wondered how to disciple all the new converts. "Let's try to strengthen our new believers class," one pastor suggested. "No, let's invigorate our Sunday School," another mentioned. This routine continued for months with practically no fruit. We were caught in a game of musical chairs in which newcomers replaced those who departed, often without explanation.

Beyond the problem of losing new converts, we earned the reputation as a cold, unloving church. Our emphasis on weeklong campaigns brought forth many converts, but our regular members were disgruntled. "I don't feel like I belong," complained one. "No one greets me in this church," another simmered. We heard these complaints often but chose to focus on the positive. Many were receiving Christ through our church. We were one of the larger churches in Ecuador, a land where only 3.5 percent of the population knows Jesus Christ.

In the midst of revolving membership and a growing reputation for coldness, we initiated cell ministry. We focused on cell leaders who would care for the flock. In less than two years, the cells grew from the initial five among the university students to 51. Each homogeneous department soon wanted to organize itself around cell ministry. Warmth and love replaced the coldness. We also slammed shut the back door, and celebration attendance skyrocketed from 550 to 950. Surely, we were experiencing a relationship between cell growth and church growth.

Cell ministry is the most effective way to close a church's back door. Concentrate on your cell ministry. Cell ministry grows pew-sitters into pastors who care for the flock. New believers are converted into leaders who continue the process.

EFFECTIVE PASTORING THAT
SHARES RESPONSIBILITY

"You pray pastor. You're getting paid for it." Even now I chuckle at this response to Chuck Smith (Calvary Chapel of Costa Mesa, California) by a former member of his congregation. Not every layperson overtly expresses such sentiments, but many quietly think them. Doesn't the Bible say that the pastor should fulfill the role of priest, prophet, pastor, and janitor? Carl George calls this the "mom and pop" mentality. Just as the "mom and pop" stores sold a little of everything, the "mom and pop" pastor must do everything.[3]

In most churches today, a staff pastor manages all the caring. Is someone sick? The pastor is expected at the hospital to pray. Does someone need counseling? The pastor is waiting in his office. Is there a church committee meeting? It wouldn't be the same without the pastor present. In this model, the church grows only to the level of the pastor's capacity to meet the congregation's needs. The pastor can do only so much. He can disciple only so many newcomers, for example. The rest fall through the cracks and eventually slip out the back door.

God is revealing to His church that the day of the one-man-show is over. Many pastors realize that they can get the job accomplished only by working through others. Take, for example, the difference between a rancher and a shepherd. A rancher hires people to care for the sheep. All of the sheep receive care, but through a wider distribution of administration. The rancher cares for the sheep by supervising and training the shepherds (small group leaders).

Compare the role of the shepherd with that of the rancher:

CHARACTERISTICS OF SHEPHERDS[4]	CHARACTERISTICS OF RANCHERS
1. Primary caregiving — "How can I meet this need?" 2. Overestimated significance — "Without me, nothing will get done" 3. Expectation drivenness — "Everyone is expecting me to get the job accomplished" 4. Availability — "How can I be more accessible to the church?" 5. Performance — "Everything depends on me" 6. Poor delegating ability — "No one can do it quite like me"	1. Ministry to the needs of the congregation through training group leaders 2. Flexible supervision 3. Focus on the outcome 4. Enable people to function without them 5. Skilled in management

The rancher cares for the shepherds who care for the sheep. The rancher ensures the sheep are tended, but he doesn't do it himself. Like the rancher who works through hired hands, effective pastors work through small-group leaders to extend themselves throughout the entire church. They ensure the shepherds are trained, prepared, and receive the necessary attention.

Paul the apostle was concerned with this principle when he wrote about the five-fold ministry: "It was he who gave some to be apostles, some to be prophets, some to be evangelists, and some to be pastors and teachers, to prepare God's people for works of service, so that the body of Christ may be built up" (Eph. 4:11-12). The job of Christian leadership is to make room for the harvest by preparing God's people for works of service.

Moses learned this lesson the hard way. Moses tried to pastor the multitude by himself. He did everything possible to take care of them on his own, but to no avail. His father-in-law, Jethro, counseled Moses to raise up leaders to care for the thousands, hundreds, and tens of people. Moses overcame his challenge by delegating leadership to others and developing small groups to care for the people.

One pastor cannot even adequately minister or provide care to a group of 50 to 100. George says, "What actually transpires is a limited intimacy and a limited accountability. Over time, many people grow dissatisfied and disillusioned, not understanding why it's so hard to go deeper in feelings of caring and belonging."[5]

It's similar to the age-old problem of oversized classrooms. No matter how superb the teacher, the students don't receive adequate personal attention. There is a size problem. The department-program model church doesn't address this concern. Certain people invariably receive more attention than others. Those who are naturally outgoing approach the pastor and even develop a relationship with him. But the majority of his flock receives little attention.

When a Christian leader captures the vision of focusing on under-shepherds (cell leaders) to pastor the rest of the congregation, proper personal care results. The sheep are again satisfied and the church can continue to grow.

COMPETENT COUNSELING THAT UTILIZES LAYPEOPLE

Think of a church as a hospital full of wounded people. Some hospitals (clinics) offer short-term care, while others have both short- and long-term. What kind of hospital is your church?

Take counseling ministries, for example. Many counseling ministries fail to disciple and mentor those counseled. The needy person arrives for his or her appointment, receives some help and encouragement, and returns the following week. But what happens — or doesn't happen — afterward is the deficient point in most church-oriented counseling ministries. Long-term counseling, in other words, falters over time. The wounds may heal, but counselors offer little preventative medicine.

What if small-group leaders are the counselors? Wouldn't that arrangement produce greater long-term results? Counselors in that situation can dispense preventative medicine as well as prescriptive. A cell leader ministers to specific needs but then invites the person to the cell group and to a discipling relationship for further growth.

I understand the place and necessity of professional counseling. Some people suffer inordinate phobias, childhood problems and difficulties that require special treatment. Every church leader should know how to contact reliable, godly specialists. But the majority of problems can be ministered to effectively through trained cell-group leaders and members.

EFFICIENT ADMINISTRATION THAT SIMPLIFIES MINISTRY

Cell-church ministry simplifies church administration, because everything is overseen through the cell system. We at the Republic Church in Quito, Ecuador, for example, grew tired of depending on one or two people to organize the ushers. We asked the cell zones to provide ushers on a rotating basis. This idea operated so well that we assigned the zones to provide Sunday School teachers as well. Sunday School teachers became plentiful. Is there a need for counselors to disciple those who come forward at an altar call? Use cell leaders! The 14 zones at Bethany World Prayer Center rotate weekly to provide ushers, greeters, parking attendants, altar ministers, nursery help, intercessors and any other help needed during the services that week. Then they take "off" for the next 13 weeks.[6] It makes sense.

When El Niño struck the coastal cities of Ecuador in 1998, many residents struggled without food, shelter or clothing. The Republic Church could have met these people's needs by erecting a separate program called "social services." Instead, we petitioned the cell groups to provide these necessities. Never before had our church contributed so much to meet the physical needs of hurting people. Many cell churches successfully operate through the cells to reach the social needs of their area.

My former church has a "cell ministry," but it's one ministry among many. The cell director, like all of the church's other pastors, is allocated space and attention to promote his ministry. When the pastors meet on Tuesdays, the pastor over cell ministry is allotted a certain time to share. The senior pastor listens, offers words of support to the cell director and then passes to the next ministry area. "Twenty people passed through our church for counseling," says the pastor in charge of counseling, and the senior pastor replies, "Great job." "Has anyone seen Joe in church recently?" asks the concerned youth pastor. No one has, so the next ten minutes are spent trying to figure out how to reconnect with Joe. Does this scenario sound familiar? BWPC's Larry Stockstill says:

> Program leaders all vie for the senior pastor's attention and budgetary priorities. ... The leaders all try to woo the same volunteers into their programs. Staff meetings become emotionally charged over what is truly important. The pastor is bewildered in deciding which program to give creative energy to.[7]

Pastoral ministry in the cell church is focused ministry. For example, when we at the Republic Church meet as a pastor team, each pastor talks about the progress of ministry among his or her cells. Each of us reports on pastoring, training, evangelizing, baptizing and visiting. We're all involved in the principal work of ministry, which is training laypeople how to minister.

Because of the similarity of purpose, it's easier to raise-up full-time pastors from your own congregation. Where will these pastors come from? From the cell leaders who rapidly multiply their cells, thus demonstrating their ability to evangelize, pastor, disciple, and train new leaders.

It's also easier to measure progress among staff members. For example, we begin our weekly pastoral meeting by reporting what each director of cells accomplished during the week among his or her cell groups. The cell secretary has all of these statistics compiled before the pastoral meeting. But we don't talk only about "accomplishments;" we discuss the needs of our people and then enter a time of fervent prayer.

Such a focused ministry is more efficient at pastoring the entire church. All pastors are directly caring for cell leaders, who in turn care for the sheep. All pastors are actively involved in evangelism, pastoring, training, visitation, and counseling. As a result the staff is more productive.

New Testament Christianity

We've examined church growth and cell-church benefits. We've also heard the alarm concerning the dangers of over-dependence on methodologies. Beyond the cell-church "methodology" is a philosophy that touches the very heart of the New Testament. The New Testament declares that the church of Jesus Christ is the family of God, the body of Christ, and the people of God. The cell church best experiences this New Testament imagery and helps people encounter the reality of Jesus Christ.

The Church as the Family of God

The church as God's people is closely tied to the understanding that the church is the family of God (Eph. 2:14-15). We are God's chosen people and thus have been adopted into His family, the church. Cell groups highlight this truth by meeting in homes. J. Goezmann confirms this: "What could be conveyed by the idea of the family of God had, in fact, already come into being in the primitive Christian community through the house churches."[8] We should relate to each other as members of God's family. We have been adopted into His heavenly family and therefore can honestly call each other "brothers and sisters."

Nothing confirms the fact that we are, indeed, God's family quite like the atmosphere of a home. The home adds a distinct flavor of family living (decorations, furniture, kitchen, etc.). It doesn't take long to taste and feel the presence of family relationships. In a homey atmosphere, cell members warm to each other more quickly than during a similar meeting in the church building.

Many churches try to maintain a "family feeling" in a large group. They do everything together: the family picnic, the Sunday School barbecue, the Super Bowl shin-dig, and the annual major league baseball gathering. In this type of church, most events are group events. Is there anything wrong with this? Of course not. The idea is great. The problem lies with the size.

Churches in this category don't realize that their size hinders true family fellowship. When the church was only a handful of people in the early years, such fellowship occurred. But many "family churches" have even grown to 200 people. The size of these churches now hinders fellowship. But so often the faithful still insist on large church-size events to maintain the semblance of family.

Many church bodies resist gathering in smaller groups for fear of losing control, and thus these churches seldom grow larger. Yet the only way to grow larger is to grow smaller. Martin and McIntosh say: "Whenever a congregation reaches a worship attendance of 200, it is impossible for individuals to relate as a family. Therefore, as a church gets larger, if the need for fellowship and intimacy are to be met, the congregation must be broken down into small units."[9]

When small groups are at the base of your church, there is more hope that you'll be able to sustain the growth that God wants to give you. Small groups maintain the sense of family in the church even when you continue to reach the lost and grow. It's the way to grow exponentially without losing relational quality.

The Church as the Body of Christ
The church is the body of Christ (1 Cor. 12:27). Christ, the head of the church, chooses the members of His body and every part is of equal importance (1 Cor. 12:12-26). As in the human body, each part plays a different function. How does a Christian know which part to play in the Body? In Paul's three major passages referring to the Body of Christ (Eph. 4, Rom. 12, 1 Cor. 12-14), he defines each member's part by his or her corresponding gifts.

Paul wasn't writing theories about the church as the body. In the early church, believers operated as the body of Christ by exercising their spiritual gifts as they interacted among themselves. God bestows His gifts so members of the Body can contribute to the welfare and edification of the whole.

How did everyone participate? Along with the united celebration (Acts 2:46a), we read that they also broke bread in their *homes* and ate together with glad and sincere hearts (Acts 2:46b). With this intimate atmosphere in mind, Paul wrote, "... When you come together, everyone has a hymn, or a word of instruction. ..." (1 Cor. 14:26).

The home-cell atmosphere enhances the exercise of spiritual gifts. This participatory atmosphere is being rediscovered in a fresh way through the cell-group movement. Only in the intimacy of a small, closely knit group will many Christians feel safe enough to exercise their spiritual gifts. George reminds us that, "Because of the intimate, accountability-inviting context of an affinity-based group, participants will readily accept the call of God that accompanies the discovery of their gifts."[10]

Many churchgoers are consumers, not participants. Churchgoers attend service on a special day of the week in order to receive some type of ministry. Yet congregations that stress only the Sunday service do not experience the New Testament Body of Christ, which was a participating, interacting organism. George Hunter believes that Christians who attend "church" without belonging to a small group are experiencing only half of the Christian life:

> Many people are involved in the congregation … but not in the cell; they therefore never experience half of what 'church' has to offer. Only in the church's redemptive cells do we really know each other, and support each other, and pull for each other, and draw strength from each other, and weep with each other, and rejoice with each other, and hold each other accountable, and identify each other's gifts, and experience what it means to be 'members of one another.'[11]

We live in an impersonal society where hearts cry out for individual attention. Everything is fast: fast food, fast money, fast fun. After a hard day's work, people retreat to their castles and emotionally prepare themselves for the next day of work. Few people spill over into the streets after work.

Because of our individualism, we avoid relationships and the transparency they require. Cell ministry is face-to-face ministry specifically designed to tear away layers of pain and hidden agendas. Each cell meeting should include these four steps which develop community: Welcome, Worship, Word and Witness (or Works). The icebreaker (Welcome) normally touches some part of each person's past and, while often humorous, it reveals a lot about each person. Then Worship draws the members into the presence of the living God. The cell lessons (Word) invite each person to contribute, thus avoiding the one-man-show mentality. Finally the vision-casting time (Witness) requires the group to work together to win a lost world for Christ.

In this setting, the group learns to operate as the body exercising all of the gifts.

The Church as the People of God

The apostle Paul depicts the church as the people of God. God chose a people whom He calls His church. This New Testament concept reflects the Old Testament image of God calling his people out of Egypt to enter the land that He promised to them. Paul wrote to the church in Thessalonica, "But we are bound to give thanks to God always for you, brethren beloved by the Lord, because God chose you from the beginning to be saved, through sanctification by the Spirit and belief in the truth" (2 Thes. 2:13-14).

The church as the people of God stands in direct contrast to the popular opinion that the church is an institution. The church is a living, spiritual household of God's people. We as the people of God are an organism as opposed to a building. When the early church fathers spoke of "churches," they referred to gathered communities of believers, not buildings. Archaeologists find no hint of church buildings before A.D. 150.

Yet we become so caught up in maintaining expensive buildings that we forget that the church's primary concern should be fulfilling her role as a "called out assembly of God's people." Anxious concern to utilize expensive buildings can smother the need for intimate, body-oriented gatherings. We must build and use our church buildings with this in mind: The building is there for the people, not the people for the sake of the building.

CONCLUSION

In 1961, the snowmobile was introduced among the Skolt Lapps, a reindeer-herding people of Northern Finland. By 1971, almost every one of the 72 households had at least one snowmobile, which soon replaced skis and reindeer sleds among the Skolt Lapps. Why? The benefits. Snowmobiles reduce the round trip for supplies from three days (reindeer sled) to five hours (snowmobile) and make it much easier to herd reindeer.[12]

You might be reading about the cell church for the first time. "What's in it for me?" and "How can cell ministry make a positive difference in my church?" are appropriate questions. The cell-church model will increase your effectiveness in evangelism, pastoring, counseling, administration, and experiencing the vital life and community of New Testament Christianity.

Are you ready to change your paradigm?

6

FOLLOW

THE EARLY CHURCH

The heart of the early church was the home-cell movement. The Holy Spirit, working through the cell-based church, ignited an explosion we are experiencing anew today. What kind of structure did God employ?

- Acts 2:46: "Every day they continued to meet together in the temple courts. They broke bread in their homes and ate together with glad and sincere hearts."
- Acts 5:42: "Day after day, in the temple courts and from house to house, they never stopped teaching and proclaiming the Good News that Jesus is the Christ." They experienced the thrill of the throngs and the intimacy of the few.
- Acts 16:5 reveals the results: "So the churches were strengthened in the faith and grew daily in numbers." Many Christians are so excited about the cell-church system because of its strong biblical base.

CHRIST AND SMALL GROUPS

The apostles experienced the power of small groups during their years with the Master. After Jesus filled them with the Holy Spirit and released them to build His church, the disciples naturally implemented the structure Christ had modeled for them. Through the small group, they became intimately acquainted with Jesus and with each other. Despite their obvious differences — a tax collector, a freedom fighter, a fisherman — they grew to love each other. Jesus performed miracles in His small group, then lectured on their meaning. He taught obscure parables to the multitudes but repeatedly and patiently clarified their meaning for His small group. Jesus modeled the way of truth, and the disciples observed and tasted this in their small group.

The 12 understood godly community better than anyone. When the apostle John wrote to the first-century Christians about community (*koinonia*), he shared from experience. Powerful transformations certainly occurred as Christ's followers interacted with their Master in this small-group environment.

FIRST-CENTURY CELLS AND CELEBRATION

As the apostles applied the church structure they understood, they brought the believers together in large gatherings and instructed them to meet in small, intimate groups. With no building to house the first Christians, they worshiped in Jewish temples and ministered to each other from house to house (Acts 2:46). Paul the apostle, although not one of the original 12, followed the same pattern. After years of ministry, he reiterated his strategy to the Ephesian elders, "You know that I have not hesitated to preach anything that would be helpful to you but have taught you publicly and from house to house" (Acts 20:20).

Need for both Cell and Celebration

Cell churches today meet weekly for both cell and celebration. But the early church gathered daily. "Day after day, in the temple courts and from house to house, they never stopped teaching and proclaiming the Good News that Jesus is the Christ" (Acts 5:42).

The ecstasy of the large celebration and the closeness of small-group fellowship fed the early church with a varied but stable diet. The believers heard timeless teachings and rejoiced in vibrant celebration. They recognized that they were experiencing something huge and dynamic. Yet the masses felt secure because of the intimate relationships developed by gathering with a few "regulars." Thus the powerful dynamic of the cell church was born. Both cell and celebration were essential in those early days because of the practical benefits each offered.

Benefits of Celebration

In the celebration, God appointed gifted teachers to feed the entire flock on His Word, otherwise regarded as devoting themselves to the "apostles' teaching" (Acts 2:42). How exhilarating it must have been to hear from the very apostles who had walked hand-in-hand with Jesus for three years. The early Jewish believers required clear teaching relating the Messiah's teaching to the Old Testament. With enemies within and without poised to pounce on the fragile church, those believers needed a firm foundation. During those celebration meetings, the apostles also imparted the vision to take the Gospel to the ends of the world. After all, the commission of the Master was to disciple all nations.

Benefits of Cell

But the celebration alone was inadequate for the early church, which required a channel for expressing the vital life of the Holy Spirit.

Taking in God's power without having an outlet for it brings stagnation. The apostles' teaching would have grown cold and impersonal without a way to apply it. God provided such participation in the small house groups. After hearing the Word of God, the believers carried those principles to the home meetings. Discussion, participation and ministry flowed naturally from the teachings. Each member exercised spiritual gifts for the edification of the Body of Christ. The one gathering complimented the other. Unlike the large masses in the temple courts who heard the Word of God from the apostles, the small, home-cell groups were personal and application-oriented.

HOUSE-CHURCH MOVEMENT

In the early part of the first century, the celebration/cell experience occurred on a daily basis. Persecution, however, eventually rendered such meetings impossible as the wrath of the Roman legions crashed down upon the early Christians. The authorities hauled many believers to jail and some even to death. We read that "… Herod the king stretched forth his hands to vex certain of the church. He had James, the brother of John, put to death with the sword" (Acts 12:1-2). Christianity soon became an underground movement. The logical meeting place was private homes, not the public temples.

Peter, for example, was fleeing persecution when he arrived at the house of Mary the mother of John, "… where many people had gathered and were praying" (Acts 12:12). Home cells were already a way of life, but now they became the sole gathering of the church. The believers combined cell and celebration times in those early house meetings, and the house church became normative.

The cell/celebration paradigm was preferred until persecution made it impossible, and this fact holds implications for today's cell church. When possible, it's preferable to offer both cell and celebration. These two types of meetings provide the spiritual fiber essential to every believer. The house-church model (independent churches meeting in homes) makes sense in places like China and other restricted-access countries where Christians are not permitted to gather for official "church" services.[1]

Some point out that the early house churches met occasionally for celebration gatherings even during the persecution of Christians. The Love Feast of 1 Corinthians 11 and Paul's visit to Troas in Acts 20:6-12 could be examples of joint celebrations. Bruce comments, "Such house churches appear to have been smaller circles of fellowship within the larger fellowship of the city *ecclesia*."[2] Paul also serves glimpses of this relationship in his epistles. "To the church of God in Corinth, to those sanctified in Christ Jesus" he writes to the citywide church (1 Cor. 1:1). "Aquila and Priscilla greet you warmly in the Lord, and so does the church that meets at their house." Here Paul writes about a specific house church (1 Cor. 16:19). Paul repeats this pattern in his epistles to the Thessolonians and the Romans (1 Th. 1:1, 2 Th. 1:1, Rom. 16:23). Robert Banks, a New Testament scholar with expertise on house churches, acknowledges that Paul often implied a relationship between house churches, although not through any ecclesiastical polity.[3]

NEW TESTAMENT CONTEXT

We all have the tendency to read our present church structures into the New Testament. For example, some reading the communion passages will imagine Paul standing behind a table in a 200-seat first-century church because that's what their pastor does today. They may forget that Paul wrote the epistles as letters to specific house churches. Here are some examples of passages written to house churches:

1. Acts 12:12 — "When this had dawned on (Peter), he went to the house of Mary the mother of John, also called Mark, where many people had gathered and were praying."

2. Romans 16:3-5 — "Greet Priscilla and Aquila, my fellow workers in Christ Jesus. They risked their lives for me. Not only I but all the churches of the Gentiles are grateful to them. Greet also the church that meets at their house."

3. 1 Corinthians 16:19 — "The churches in the province of Asia send you greetings. Aquila and Priscilla greet you warmly in the Lord, and so does the church that meets at their house."

4. Colossians 4:15 — "Give my greetings to the brothers at Laodicea, and to Nympha and the church in her house."

5. Philemon 2 — "Apphia our sister, to Archippus our fellow soldier and to the church that meets in your home ..."

All of the New Testament letters were written to the first-century house churches. When Paul, for example, wrote about believers serving each other and waiting on each other during the Lord's Supper, it was in the context of a home, not of a church building. When Paul expounded on the operation of spiritual gifts, he referred to a house-church environment. When he clarified the role of each member in the body of Christ, he pictured the warm atmosphere of the early house church. John Mallison writes, "It is almost certain that every mention of a local church or meeting, whether for worship or fellowship, is in actual fact a reference to a church meeting in a house."[4] Hadaway, S. Wright and DuBose add, "From the beginning, homes appeared to be the place for the most enduring dimensions of early church life."[5] Place the following scriptural occurrences within the atmosphere of the first-century house church:

1. The Lord's Supper: 1 Corinthians 11:18,20,23 — "In the first place, I hear that when you come together as a church, there are divisions among you, and to some extent I believe it. When you come together, it is not the Lord's Supper you eat ... for I received from the Lord what I also passed on to you: The Lord Jesus, on the night he was betrayed, took bread, and when he had given thanks, he broke it and said, 'This is my body, which is for you; do this in remembrance of me.' In the same way, after supper he took the cup, saying, 'This cup is the new covenant in my blood; do this, whenever you drink it, in remembrance of me.' For whenever you eat this bread and drink this cup, you proclaim the Lord's death until he comes ..."

2. The Body of Christ: 1 Corinthians 12:14, 22, 25, 27 — "Now the body is not made up of one part but of many. If the foot should say, 'Because I am not a hand, I do not belong to the body,' it would not for that reason cease to be part of the body. On the contrary, those parts of the body that seem to be weaker are indispensable, so that there should be no division in the body, but that its parts should have equal concern for each other. If one part suffers, every part suffers with it; if one part is honored, every part rejoices with it. Now you are the body of Christ, and each one of you is a part of it."

3. The Gifts of the Spirit: Romans 12:5-8 — "... So in Christ we who are many form one body, and each member belongs to all the others. We have different gifts, according to the grace given us. If a man's gift is prophesying, let him use it in proportion to his faith. If it is serving, let him serve; if it is teaching, let him teach; if it is encouraging, let him encourage; if it is contributing to the needs of others, let him give generously; if it is leadership, let him govern diligently; if it is showing mercy, let him do it cheerfully."

4. Priesthood of All Believers: Revelations 1:5-6: — "... And from Jesus Christ, who is the faithful witness, the firstborn from the dead, and the ruler of the kings of the earth. To him who loves us and has freed us from our sins by his blood, and has made us to be a kingdom and priests to serve his God and Father — to him be glory and power for ever and ever! Amen."

5. Caring for One Another: Ephesians 4:32; 5:1-2 — "Be kind and compassionate to one another, forgiving each other, just as in Christ God forgave you. ... Be imitators of God, therefore, as dearly loved children and live a life of love, just as Christ loved us and gave himself up for us as a fragrant offering and sacrifice to God."

6. Hospitality: 1 Peter 4:8-9; 3:8 — "Above all, love each other deeply, because love covers over a multitude of sins. Offer hospitality to one another without grumbling. ... Finally, all of you, live in harmony with one another; be sympathetic, love as brothers, be compassionate and humble."

7. Social Action: Romans 15:25-26 — "Now, however, I am on my way to Jerusalem in the service of the saints there. For Macedonia and Achaia were pleased to make a contribution for the poor among the saints in Jerusalem."

The warm, caring atmosphere of the house church prevailed for about four centuries. The world tried desperately to annihilate Christ's church through torture, terror and endless persecution, but the church clung to its Lord while meeting underground. They grew remembering the words of Peter 1:6-8:

> In this you greatly rejoice, though now for a little while you may have had to suffer grief in all kinds of trials. These have come so that your faith — of greater worth than gold, which perishes even though refined by fire — may be proved genuine and may result in praise, glory and honor when Jesus Christ is revealed.

Despite fierce persecution, the early church grew exponentially. The mighty Roman Empire couldn't stop Jesus' believers, and

Christianity soon conquered the world. Jesus, the Lord of the Church, granted victory. Satan would have fared better against a large, centralized church. But because he had to war against scattered house churches meeting throughout the empire, his task proved futile.

Then a cataclysmic shift unexpectedly occurred, and the church emerged a public hero. The era of emperor Constantine ushered in a whole new church dynamic.

THE SHIFT AWAY FROM EARLY CHURCH PRINCIPLES

When Emperor Constantine rose to power (A.D. 312), he granted the church rest from continual persecution. In so many ways, this was a tremendous victory. Why then did the church enter a period called the "dark ages"? Here are a few of the many reasons:

The Legalization of Christianity

Constantine promised to forgo persecution, so Christianity was no longer the forbidden religion. But he then instated Christianity as the state religion. The old order was suddenly reversed.

When Christianity was a despised and outlawed religion, only the true believers participated in the affairs of the church. With Christianity's resounding acceptance, everyone ran to join. "If you can't beat them, you might as well join them" became the sentiment of the times. Whole armies were baptized in one fell swoop. People converted from pagan religions to Christianity because it was the culturally acceptable thing to do. The world became part of the church, and the church became part of the world.

Constantine went so far as to place priests on government salary. The once lowly Christian church became the high-minded state church, going from riches to rags overnight. "Worldly" Christians comprised a large group in the church. But all of these seemingly positive events carried the heavy price tag of undercutting spirituality and zeal for the purity of the Gospel. Sacred Christian fellowship turned into impersonal religious ritual.

The Priesthood of all Special Saints

Various factors were working behind the scenes to widen the gap between clergy and laity. The spontaneity and priesthood of all believers came under stricter control of the elected bishops.

Since New Testament Scripture was still emerging, many voices clamored for authority and claimed the truth. How could one differentiate the true church from the legions of religious alternatives (e.g., Gnosticism, etc.)? "Apostolic succession," which granted authority to those who could trace their origin to the original apostles, became the way to distinguish between those who had God's authority and those who did not. Kenneth Scott Latourette explains,

> He [Irenaeus] ... was emphatic that the apostles had appointed as successors bishops to whom they had committed the churches. ... These bishops had been followed by others in unbroken line who were also guardians and guarantors of the apostolic teaching. He hints that he could, if there were space, give the lists of the bishops of all the churches, but he singles out that of the Church of Rome. ...[6]

Those in authority developed elaborate lists to prove that such-and-such a person was indeed a disciple of a disciple of someone who knew the earlier apostles. Only a successor of an apostle could rightfully minister. Constantine publicly acknowledged and recompensed these bishops. The church began to esteem this "inheritance" more than a person's piety and anointing. In major cities, bishops grew in power, and their word was respected and obeyed.

Ministry became the exclusive, personal job of select ministers. Only the chosen could rightfully minister to the multitude. These special saints held center stage, while the ordinary Christian was expected to sit, listen, and obey. This resulted in the inactivity of the laity. The Bible was taken from the hands of the people and given to those learned men who would study it and offer their judgments. William Brown writes:

> The reversion to an 'official' priesthood or ministry ... cast the laity chiefly into the role of hearers of the Law and spectators of the mysterious tableau of the sacrifices. This passive role in worship became once more the normal experience of the people of God as the church developed.[7]

This cast system of hierarchy killed lay initiative because personal innovation and freedom were discouraged. Submission and obedience were demanded. As the hierarchical machine strengthened, it implemented torturous methods to prevent laypeople from expounding on biblical ideas. Strict order and maintenance of the status quo were significant activities.

Many Old Testament rituals were woven into the Mass, and the priests interacted little with the people. How foreign such behavior would have been to the early house churches! Sunday liturgy replaced the small-group sharing so common in the daily gatherings of the early house churches. As the huge basilicas were erected, the life of the church and the Body of Christ crashed downward.

The doctrine of the priesthood of all believers quickly faded. The early church embraced any man or women of God who ministered in power, and leaders were appointed according to their particular gifting. But the state church required Christians to pass through all the procedures and trappings of the priesthood before releasing them to ministry. These words of Peter became foreign:

> "But you are a chosen people, a royal priesthood, a holy nation, a people belonging to God, that you may declare the praises of him who called you out of darkness into his wonderful light. Once you were not a people, but now you are the people of God; once you had not received mercy, but now you have received mercy" (1 Peter 2:9-10).

Demise of the House Church

With the advent of Constantine and the legalization of Christianity, immense and lavish temples were built from government coffers. These impressive works of art, with their ornaments and images, may even have given the uninitiated a sense of God's majesty, but at a high price: The house, the badge and identity of the early church, became unnecessary and irrelevant.[8] Celebration without cell became the accepted means of worship. The life that characterized the early church seeped away in the cold temples of the Middle Ages. If only they could have found the balance of the New Testament structure!

Yet among the pomp and luxury of those cathedral gatherings, many seeking souls longed for more. A severe dichotomy developed between the super-spiritual and the religious majority. Those who yearned for more of God felt compelled to separate from the ceremony and trappings of the Mass. These earnest people fled to the mountains and deserts to seek the living God, and they found refuge in monasteries and mountain hideouts. But in their search for a New Testament church, they separated from the rest of the body. This was never God's plan. The cell/celebration paradigm fizzled, and the church stumbled into the dark ages.

THE REFORMATION

Thankfully, the Reformation occurred. Along with the liberating doctrine of justification, which declares people free of the guilt and the penalty attached to sin because of Jesus' sacrifice, Martin Luther declared anew that all believers were priests before God (1 Peter 2:9-10).

Luther concluded that the Roman See was separating the people from God by emphasizing hierarchy and position. The doctrine of justification called everyone to stand before God through Christ. The whole church was called to live by faith before God and perform the activity of priests before God. This calling was not just for a chosen few, but for the whole church.

Luther and the Priesthood of All Believers

Luther did not take the Reformation far enough. While Luther emphasized correct doctrine, his affect on church structure was minimal. Positively, many were awakened to their own responsibility before God, and the preaching of the Word again became central. Luther, however, believed that the church consisted of the entire state, which a person entered through infant baptism. Everyone in the state was considered part of the church and required to attend Sunday services.

Luther's Resistance of Home Groups

In the early days of the Reformation, Luther spoke highly of small groups. He even wrote about the possibility that "… those who want to be Christians in earnest … should sign their names and meet alone in a house somewhere to pray, to read, to baptize, to receive the sacrament, and to do other Christian works."[9]

Yet that was before the Anabaptists, who practiced baptism of adult believers. They worshiped in "gathered" churches, not identical with the community at large but composed of those who had experienced new birth. The Reformation church strongly opposed their activity.

With the Anabaptist controversy on his mind, Luther confessed that he had "changed his mind," stating that he no longer believed that "earnest Christians" should meet together in the home "to pray, to read, to baptize, to receive the sacrament, and to do other Christian works …"[10] Luther feared the potential divisiveness of small groups. He wrote,

> All the elements [of the true church] would be there in these small groups and, as sure as Satan seeks to destroy our souls, some Pharisaical spirit will conclude that his little group is the church, and that everyone outside is damned. Indeed, it has already happened, if I am to believe the rumor I hear. Certain false brethren rebaptize themselves and then sneak away from God's church to meet with other misled fools in various holes and corners. They claim that they are the only true Christians, and teach that they must separate from all iniquity.[11]

Luther's concerns were practical and pragmatic. He had enough opposition from the Roman Catholic Church, so why make the Reformation even more radical by separating from the state church structure? Luther's movement depended on the state's protection from Rome. Allowing the Anabaptists to separate from the state was paramount to weakening the unity of the state.

A RETURN TO BIBLICAL ROOTS

Since the time of Luther, several movements have attempted to recapture the New Testament home movement: Martin Bucer and the reformation movement in Salzburg, the Pietistic movement, the Moravian movement, the Methodist movement, and now the modern cell movement. These movements went beyond the Reformation church to practicing the priesthood of all believers.

There is a new awakening to return to the New Testament paradigm of cell-celebration. Cell groups lack significance if they're not connected with praise and worship. The worship celebration can grow as large as possible — the bigger the better! It's like watching a professional basketball game. The largeness of the crowd contributes to the excitement. J.I. Packer writes: "... I go around telling people that if they're not with the whole congregation on Sunday, and in the small group somewhere during the week, their Christian lives are unbalanced."[12]

Instead, many Christians hop from the huge Sunday crowd to a large Bible study or department meeting. It's smaller, but it's not intimate. Others prefer to hide under the droning of a pastor's sermon. These churchgoers dart quickly to the exit door and avoid all personal contact. Content with having "done their duty," they ease their conscience until the next Sunday rolls around.

An increasing number are coming to grips with their dual responsibility. People must participate in a large celebration, but they also need to belong to something small enough that it touches their personal buttons. Everyone needs a chance to express the "real me," and no one can tell it quite like you. You are a unique individual full of emotions, victories, problems, and pain. And like anything complex, your system can break down and go haywire unless it's cared for and fine-tuned. This is the role of the cell group. People in Christ's church are longing for personal attention.

The beauty of the small group within the church structure is the equilibrium between the small and the large — the roar of the crowd and the listening ear of the cell. Both are important. Only on the cell level can people's deeply felt needs be met. Rick Warren, founder of one of the largest churches in the U.S. (over 10,000 people attend Saddleback each Sunday) says,

> One of the biggest fears members have about growth is how to maintain that 'small church' feeling or fellowship as their church grows. The antidote to this fear is to develop small groups within your church. … Our church must always be growing larger and smaller at the same time. … Large group's celebrations give people the feeling that they are part of something significant. But you can't share personal prayer requests in the crowd. Small affinity groups, on the other hand, are perfect for creating a sense of intimacy and close fellowship. It's there that everybody knows your name. When you are absent, people notice.[13]

Today's cell-church movement is rekindling the fire of the early church. There is a new hunger for something more than a congregational gathering. There is a wellspring of hope as God calls His church to look backward in order to march forward. This "backward look" clarifies the early church dynamic. The early church evangelized so effectively because it developed spiritual muscles in the warmth of Christian community.

STRUCTURE YOUR
CHURCH FOR GROWTH

7

Understand the
Cell Itself

No matter what kind of small group you are searching for, you probably can find it. Small groups exist in the United States for people with physical disorders, youth with chemical dependency, singles, couples having problems, and parents of children with learning disorders. The list continues. Eighty million of the 200 million adults in the U.S. are in a small group.[1] One out of six of them is a new member, thus confirming that small groups are alive and growing.[2]

But what is a small group? With the proliferation of so many types of small groups, confusion clouds the horizon. Some define small groups as anything that is small and a group. This might include Sunday School classes, the board meeting, the choir, or a home-cell group. Various small-group models dot the North American landscape.

Today's wide variety of small-group models offer different ways to organize your church. But all are not created equally. Some lay a better foundation than others. A word of caution: Never simply copy a small-group model. Learn the principles behind the model, and these will guide you in your situation, culture and context. Never forget that the principles are the key, and not the models that we find throughout the world. The principles bring life, direction and wisdom.

CELL CHURCH MODEL

A cell church is a non-traditional form of church life in which small groups of Christians (cells) meet in their homes to build each other up in Christ and to evangelize the unsaved. It is a church that defines its cells as the basic building blocks of church life.

Chapter 3 of this book describes important patterns and principles found in the most eminent cell churches. Most people attribute the origin of the Cell Church Model to David Yonggi Cho, whose system has been replicated by pastors and church leaders all over the world. One of the similarities among cell churches in Latin America, for example, is Cho's influence on their cell ministry. Top cell experts such as Ralph Neighbour Jr., Carl George and Dale Galloway all liberally quote Cho as the foundation for their particular model of cell ministry.[3]

Although Cho is the primary inspiration behind the Cell Church Model, Neighbour has written the most extensively on it. He also has completed the most research on cell-based churches worldwide. His zeal and purity is evident: " ... the cell is the church, and the church is the cell. It is the basic building block of the larger community called "local church." There must be no competition with it — none at all."[4]

In the Cell Church Model, cells are the base of the church. Lawrence Khong, the pastor of one of the fastest growing cell churches, writes: "There is a vast difference between a church with cells and a cell church. ... All things the church must do ... are done through the cell. Our Sunday service is just the corporate celebration."[5] Unlike the House Church Movement, those in the cell church are committed to cell and celebration. There is a very high percentage of congregational attendance in both cell and celebration.

Cell churches emphasize the components of the cell. Cell evangelism is accomplished as a group and the goal is rapid multiplication. Because of the rapid multiplication there is the urgency of ongoing equipping and training of new leadership.

Other characteristics of the cell church include strong administrative control (required reports, Jethro model), few programs apart from cells, and active leadership involvement of the senior pastor and other staff members.

META MODEL

This model is introduced in Carl George's first book dedicated to cell ministry, *Prepare Your Church for the Future* (1991). The Meta Model is an adaptation of the Cell Church Model for the North American church and originally was patterned after the small-group ministry at the New Hope Community Church in Portland Oregon.

George reasons that small-group ministry has worked so effectively in large, growing churches that it should be adapted to work in any size church, anywhere in the world. He explains that our current models of church ministry do not provide sufficient quality care to sustain a growing church.[6] The clear, overriding focus is on the cell group which emphasizes both pastoral care and evangelism.[7]

Prepare Your Church for the Future impacted the North American church scene so powerfully because George gives fresh, North American terminology to the cell-based concepts that have worked so well overseas. There is no doubt that George is setting forth a new model of ministry for the church in North America and around the world.

In his 1994 book *The Coming Church Revolution*, George seems to redefine his so-called Meta Model. He talks about a way of analyzing churches:

> Meta-Church thinking examines the degree to which a church has been 'cellularized,' and its leadership linked. ... It tries to discern the degree to which group leaders are in fact convening their people, and the degree to which coaches are in fact working with group leaders. The Meta-Church, then, ... is an X-ray to help you look at what you have in order to figure out what's missing.[8]

In other words, instead of promoting a certain model, George says that he is providing the church a way to discern small-group involvement and how (or whether) they are moving toward a purer cell-group approach. George insists throughout his book that the Meta approach is simply a way of seeing (X-ray machine) what you already have.

George defines a small group to include: Sunday School classes, ministry teams, outreach teams, worship-production teams, sports teams, recovery groups, and more. He writes, "... any time sixteen or fewer people meet together, you have a small-group meeting."[9] He says of Sunday Schools, "The phrase 'cell groups' refers to an encompassing care system that includes Sunday School. A Sunday School is simply a centralized, on-premises cell system. Churches should have as many Sunday Schools as they can afford."[10] Commenting on the Meta Model, David Limiero writes, "The key to understanding George's model is recognizing that your church *already* has existing small groups. These groups might be Sunday School classes, the choir, elders, committees, women's circles, etc."[11]

I studied six leading churches characterized by the Meta Model[12] and discovered the following patterns.

Variety of Groups

Clearly, a variety of groups is one of the most common characteristics of these Meta churches. Following the teaching of George, these churches feature a plethora of small groups. In fact, just about any type of small group is considered acceptable: married couples over 50, drama groups, lawn-mowing groups, parking lot attendant groups, cancer groups, staging groups, sports groups, Vietnam Veteran groups, and more. Normally the various groups can be categorized into specific types or purposes, although certain Meta Models are so varied that they are hard to classify.[13] Three types of groups that most frequently surface in the Meta Churches are:

GROUP TYPE	FOCUS
TASK GROUPS	A PARTICULAR MINISTRY
FELLOWSHIP GROUPS	CARE FOR ONE ANOTHER
DISCIPLESHIP GROUPS	SPIRITUAL GROWTH

Task groups, for example, are the "bread-and-butter" small groups at Willow Creek Community Church.[14] These groups meet to accomplish some ministry program in the church (e.g., ushering, money counting, etc.), but at the same time are designed to include spiritual elements such as Bible study and prayer.

Flexibility

Leadership in these Meta churches stresses the value of flexibility. Freedom of choice is highly esteemed and emphasized, and top leaders are careful not to assert too much pressure to conform. This flexibility can be seen in at least three major areas:

1. Meetings can be held any day at any location. Many small groups at Willow Creek arrive at church 90 minutes before their church activity and meet in their groups.
2. Leaders are free to choose their own material. Saddleback Community Church gives complete freedom in this, while Willow Creek asks only that leaders obtain their material from the church's bookstore.
3. Multiplication seems to be a desired ideal in the Meta system, but it is not enforced. Again, the strong emphasis on freedom of choice precludes any type of pressure for the groups to multiply. One staff person at Saddleback Church shared that several of the small groups have been meeting for 10 years.[15] Most evangelism is accomplished through the celebration services, and small groups are a way to care for the new Christians. Some groups go on indefinitely, while others may last a few weeks. Again, it depends on the purpose of the group or the vision of the leader.

Jethro Model

These six major Meta Model churches exercise administrative control over their small groups through a loosely knit Jethro system. The "Jethro Model" refers to the counsel Jethro gave to Moses in Exodus 18. Each cell leader has someone to whom he or she is accountable. That person (called by various titles) is assigned to oversee no more than five cell leaders. Over the leader of five is another leader to whom the leader of five is accountable, and the process continues.

How many times must the upper leadership visit those under them? Again, the buzzword "flexibility" was often used. At Saddleback Community Church, for example, the district lay pastors are encouraged to visit the cell leaders every quarter.

Each of these churches also employs some type of ongoing leadership training, but the systems are flexible and changing. Willow Creek tried to gather the coaches (leaders of five small-group leaders) every month. The Cincinnati Vineyard and Fairhaven Alliance maintained a monthly leadership meeting but found it very difficult to train such a wide variety of cell leadership.

SERENDIPITY MODEL

The chief proponent of the Serendipity Model is Lyman Coleman, whose publishing house is a key resource for small-group material throughout the U.S.[16] This model of small groups can work within or outside the church. In this model, small groups meet for a season, break up and form new groups. It promotes open groups, in which new people are free to enter at any point.

Coleman was especially influenced by Sam Shoemaker, pastor of Calvary Episcopal Church in New York City. Shoemaker believed that all people around his church were his parish. His church grew in its vision to reach the entire parish, and this vision greatly influenced Coleman.[17]

This model is best understood by the characteristics that distinguish it from other models:

1. Integrated. There is a place for all kinds of groups in the church. This model can also include traditional Sunday School, where people who are already involved can find a place for sharing and caring. As small-group possibilities, Coleman mentions board meetings, choir groups, usher groups, care groups, and sports groups. In this respect, it resembles the Meta Model.

2. Collegiate system. This approach is similar to the old Sunday School system in which exists a definite departure from one

class and entrance into another class. "This model has a two-semester structure, with 'kick offs' twice a year and closure at the end of each semester. There is also a graduation/celebration at the end of the year."[18]

3. Definite beginning and end. Although Coleman's earlier models consisted of shorter time periods, he now suggests one year. He says, "The end is marked by a period of releasing where everyone responds to his new calling."[19]

A recent example of this pattern is the New Life Church in Colorado Springs, Colorado (Ted Haggard, senior pastor). The small groups in this church, called "Free Market Cells," last one semester and then the members are given a choice to continue or to find another cell.[20]

In the Serendipity approach, small-group multiplication is mentioned as a possible option. Coleman, however, believes that the Meta Model overemphasizes multiplication. He mentions that such rapid multiplication interrupts the group-building process by "splitting cells to create new cells."[21]

COVENANT MODEL

Roberta Hestenes[22] is the chief spokesperson for the Covenant Model, which mainly promotes spiritual growth among believers. Hestenes defines this model as: "A Christian group is an intentional face-to-face gathering of 3 to 12 people on a regular time schedule with the common purpose of discovering and growing in the possibilities of the abundant life in Christ."[23]

These are closed groups of Christians who meet for mutual edification. At the beginning of each group, a covenant is made which lays down the group's rules. "Covenant" refers to the commitments or promises that were established in the Old Testament between God and His people. The group makes a commitment (covenant) to fulfill particular goals, purposes, study topics, ground rules, and logistical details.[24]

Groups do not normally multiply in this approach, and one of the major goals is to create long-term community. These groups require strong commitment and a high level of accountability.[25] Although this model is strong on Christian responsibility and commitment, Coleman makes a wise observation: "Unchurched, non-Christians would not be interested in this type of group. There is no mechanism built into the system for the Covenant groups to multiply, or to close with honor. Frequently, Covenant groups will last until they die a horrible death."[26]

DEFINE YOUR SMALL GROUPS ACCURATELY

The above models demonstrate how some define small groups as anything that is small and a group. The underlying thinking is: "Give the people all the variety possible." For these teachers, a small group might be a deacon's meeting, a horseback riding club, a prison ministry task group, a choir group, and on and on the list goes. The variety of small groups is truly mind-boggling.

Now for the definition of a cell group: *A group of people (five to 15) who meet regularly for the purpose of spiritual edification and evangelistic outreach (with the goal of multiplication) and who are committed to participate in the functions of the local church.* By virtue of this definition, these small groups clearly are church-based. *Those who attend the cell groups are expected to attend the churchwide celebration as well.*

It is my conviction that not every small group is a cell group. A cell group includes certain components. Take, for example, the necessary cell components recognized by Bethany World Prayer Center: growth in relationship with God; growth in relationship with one another; growth in number, multiplication, and reaching the world with the Gospel of Jesus Christ.[27] Bethany doesn't try to label everything a cell group. If a small group at Bethany doesn't include spiritual growth and evangelistic outreach, it is not considered a cell group. The cell is defined by its characteristics and not by the fact that it is small and a group.[28] Again, the three major components of all cell groups are: seeking God (worship, prayer, lesson), developing relationships with one another (ice-breaker, ministry to one another, refreshment time), and reaching out to non-Christians (friendship evangelism, special cell activity, multiplication).

If your small group doesn't include the components of spiritual edification and evangelism (with the goal of multiplication), be honest and refuse to label it a cell group. If it's a Sunday School class, call it that! If it's a choir group, call it a choir group.

I have observed an adverse effect on the cell-based system when all small groups are embraced in the cell system and given equal priority. This mentality cheapens the cell vision by saying that a small-group usher's meeting at the church has the same priority as a home-based cell group. In fact, the two are worlds apart because of the setting and the purpose of these meetings. Lack of quality control in this smorgasbord approach eventually weakens the entire system.

I hesitate, for example, to call the worship team a cell group because it meets for a particular purpose and outsiders are not welcome. The same holds true for the church board. Can a church board evangelize and invite new people? Of course not. Concerning a sports team, how much face-to-face spiritual communion is going to take place? There is nothing wrong with Sunday School, but let's not label it an "on-campus cell system." Sunday School can play a vital teaching role in the church, but don't call it something that it's not.

Our senior pastor regularly insists that everyone in the church attend a weekly cell group so they will receive personal care and learn to reach their unbelieving neighbors. He knows they can receive through the group's pastoral care what they cannot receive in the worship service. And the cell groups are open to receive the people who hear that announcement on Sunday morning.

Yet, how could people receive pastoral care by merely joining a sports team which meets for a season, or by attending a Sunday School class which meets for a semester to study an academic subject, or by being on a committee which might meet for a month? Such gatherings are important and have their place, but they do not fulfill the purposes of a cell group. By joining a small group that isn't a cell, a person would not be pastored and often would be uncomfortable about inviting unbelieving friends. Pastors could not be assured that God's purposes were being fulfilled in the life of their members through such groups.

Cell churches concentrate on the components or characteristics of the small group and label as "cells" those groups that fit the set standard — namely, small groups of people who meet together for the purpose of mutual edification and evangelistic outreach with the goal of forming new groups.

WHAT A CELL-GROUP MEETING LOOKS LIKE

Many cell meetings, including the one I lead, follow a similar format. This is what a "typical" Thursday night cell at my home looks like.

We start with an icebreaker (the **WELCOME** segment of the meeting). We opened our meeting one week with: "If someone were to ask you a question that's guaranteed to get you talking, what would that question be?" The purpose is to literally break the ice, to ease people into fellowship with one another. We always welcome newcomers and non-Christians.

Then we seek the Lord through a time of singing and prayer (**WORSHIP**). Each person in attendance receives a song sheet. Sometimes I pick the songs, and sometimes I ask others to do this (an opportunity to get others involved in the "planning" stage). Flexibility reigns. What's important is that we enter into the presence of Jesus Christ.

Then we roll into the cell lesson (**WORD**), which should be lively and full of everyone's participation. My role is group facilitator, not Bible teacher. The cell leader is successful when all members apply the biblical passage to their own lives. My cell lesson is based on what the pastor preached the previous Sunday, and leaders receive the lesson before each sermon. During the cell lesson, God applies His Word to specific needs of those in the group. After the lesson, we share specific prayer requests and pray for one another. Often we'll lay hands on someone who is hurting.

Then we impart the vision for outreach (**WITNESS/WORKS**) to those present. I might say: "Who will you invite next week, Miguel?" or "Let's remember to pray for Paul, who will lead the next daughter cell group" or "Remember that each of you will eventually be leading a cell group, so start the training process!" We might discuss how we as a cell can gather food for those suffering the terrible affects of El Niño (this was our cell project in May 1998).

Our cell meeting lasts no longer than 90 minutes and closes with a refreshment time. Some stay for an additional hour, but others need to leave right away. Some of the most powerful ministry times occur after the cell group is dismissed, in the afterglow of God's presence.

Cells are flexible yet consistent. Some cell groups, for example, might be more "seeker-sensitive" than others. Excessive singing and prayer would not be appropriate in such meetings. We have many cell groups, for example, that meet on university campuses. Our leaders purposely try to maintain a flavor that is appropriate for that context, since the main thrust is evangelistic. Yet, even in these groups the components of knowing God and relationship-building are present.

No two cells are exactly alike but each maintains the same components: seeking God (worship, prayer, and lesson), developing relationships with one another (ice-breaker, ministry to one another, and refreshment time), and reaching out to non-Christians (friendship evangelism, special cell activity, and multiplication). These components allow cells the flexibility to be effective, while at the same time achieving their goal.

Don't Close Cells Artificially

The Serendipity Model emphasizes a beginning and an ending point. Many churches today follow this pattern and open and close their small groups every semester or year, depending on the system. The reason is to give people the liberty to "exit" and "enter" the group.

Cells, however, represent true community and shouldn't be programmed to last for a season. Cells are not like a semester-long class or Bible study. To stop and start the "train" to allow folks to "easily exit" detracts from the goal of long-term community. Granted, small groups tend to turn inward. Cell-group communion can easily turn into *koinonitus* (a church sickness). But cells avoid this problem by focusing on evangelism and multiplication. The multiplication of a cell group assures the constant flow of new life.

Develop A Strong System

Having all your church members meeting in weekly small groups is not enough, even if they are cell groups as defined in this chapter.

Cell groups need a system of support. Without proper equipping, pastoral support, vision from the senior pastor, prayer momentum, support for children's work, and weekly teaching and worship, too much pressure rests on the shoulders of the cell leader. Effective cell churches provide the needed aid to sustain the cell leader over the long haul. Let me reiterate: *Strong cell systems produce healthy cell groups.* The purpose of this book is to help you develop a growing church through a cell system that will sustain and care for your small groups over time. The following chapters provide clues to help you organize your cell system for maximum results.

8

FOCUS ON
ONE THING

Fresh out of Bible school in 1982, I became intern youth pastor at Long Beach (California) Alliance Church. I attended every meeting, volunteered for many activities and hoped to impress everyone with my willingness to serve.

During one board meeting, I said (out of habit), "I'll be glad to take on that new ministry." I thought: "I'm sure they'll jump at this opportunity to use me." After the first few positive responses, a highly respected board member, Faith Rouse, threw me a curve ball: "Joel, we appreciate your willingness to help in so many areas, but remember that you shouldn't get involved with new ministry unless you're willing to eliminate one of your current responsibilities." My nod gave the impression that I understood, but I inwardly struggled to grasp the meaning of her comment.

My good friend Faith Rouse, a seasoned Christian worker, understands human nature and me in particular: Many people tend to volunteer for new service before counting the cost of current responsibilities. She observed my propensity to divide my time and talents into a flurry of scattered activity but understood the need for me to focus on "this one thing." By helping me do a few — and just a few — things well, she was spurring me toward success.

CONCENTRATE ON "THIS ONE THING"

No one can do everything well. Therefore, a job well done requires deliberate concentration. This is true of churches, too. Successful churches cannot be all things to all people. Church growth analysts have touted this for a long time. Barna, in *User Friendly Churches*, distinguishes growing churches by their capacity to prioritize and their ability to reject what steers from their philosophy. Barna says,

> In speaking with pastors of declining churches, a common thread was their desire to do something for everybody. They had fallen into the strategic black hole of creating a ministry that looked great on paper, but had not ability to perform up to standards. Despite their worthy intentions, they tried to be so helpful to everyone that they wound up being helpful to no one.[1]

Remember that the one phrase recited in all successful cell churches is "cell ministry is the backbone of our church." The vision passed down from leaders to members is that one must belong to a cell group to receive pastoral care, because cells are the very life of the church. If your cell ministry is one more program amid endless church activity, you are bound to fail. You won't be able to concentrate on "this one thing." Too many interests will overload you. You don't want to enter cell ministry only to shelve it later, because it soon will lose its effectiveness.

Do You Run On DOS or Windows 95?

Those using personal computers may remember the DOS operating system. Windows 3.1 certainly was an improvement, but a PC needed the most recent version of DOS to run it. I discovered this the hard way. I bought a notebook computer loaded with DOS, and also WordPerfect for Windows, but I didn't buy the Windows operating system. I soon discovered that WordPerfect for Windows wouldn't run on a DOS computer system without the Windows operating system. Windows 3.1 and DOS were two operating system "layers" that wouldn't work without each other. This "latest" technology was nonetheless bulky and inadequate. Windows 95 eliminated the need for DOS because the operating system was complete.

My first "cell" ministry was much like adding Windows over DOS because it enhanced the already-existing church programs but didn't replace them. I taught seminars nationwide on how any church could *add* a small-group ministry to its structure. After all, ours helped us pastor the people better, gave leaders a place to serve, and provided better follow-up and evangelism. But we continued to maintain a wide array of church programs, resulting in constant competition for resources. The small-group ministry eventually became one program among many.

Determined to plant cells differently at the Republic Church (the daughter church), we dug deep and laid a strong cell foundation. Everything centered on cell ministry. We placed the ministry in the hands of a staff instead of just one person. We protected it against a myriad of programs, giving it the chance to grow and prosper. In this non-competitive environment, the cells grew exponentially: In just fifteen months after becoming a cell church, the number of groups skyrocketed from 21 to 117 with surprisingly little effort. Are you giving cell ministry in your church the chance to grow? Is it the church's most important ministry?

Cell ministry provides a church with a new operating platform that serves as the solid base for all activities. Through the cell system a church can pastor, evangelize, follow-up new converts, provide ushers, baptize, train, educate, raise up children's ministers, etc. It's akin to adopting a new operating system which is more complete yet simpler than the previous one. The cell system does this just as Windows 95 did for our computers.

A Church with Cells vs. a Cell Church

What is the difference between a cell church and a church with cells? A cell church organizes itself around cell ministry. In a church with cells, the cells are one ministry among many. All other ministries function as separate programs but are supposed to exist harmoniously with the small groups. One person typically heads the cell ministry, while other pastors attend to their ministries. A church with cells might emphasize the importance of cell ministry, but it is not the principle ministry.

Cell churches have two important ministries: cell and celebration. Cell ministry provides pastoral care, evangelism, counseling, follow-up, and all other important activities. The core organizational structure is based on cell ministry.

The Importance of Saying 'No'

Learning to say "no" is an important fundamental in the cell church. A million well-intentioned programs will knock, even pound, on your church door, but they will drown your cell ministry. "No" is a blessed word in the cell church. If you don't learn to say "no," your cell church system will flounder.

People attempting to help will often say, "This program will strengthen our cell ministry by making better cell leaders." Be cautious about these arguments. In one sense, every program on the market might have some long-term benefit for some cell leaders. But in the meantime, these programs draw leaders away from their primary focus and require loads of extra time. They normally benefit the cell leader only indirectly.

Don't add programs with the hope that they might benefit cell ministry in the long run. Bethany's Billy Hornsby says: "There are many good ideas that we want to attach to the cells to help them be successful. These attachments are simply not needed. In fact, they will eventually burden the cell groups so much that there will be an "overload" factor that will kill one cell group after another, along with its leadership."[2]

Admittedly, after the cell church philosophy is thoroughly implemented, other ministries might be added: television and radio ministries, for example. These do not compete with cells because everyone on staff understands where they fit. Many of the outstanding worldwide cell churches are at this point. They and others know exactly where they stand. Your cell church may reach this point some day. But to get there, you must learn to say "no."

The majority of churches are accustomed to the traditional, program style of ministry, so saying "no" is especially vital in the early stages of planting or transitioning. Until cell church ministry is a way of life, be exceedingly careful about adding programs. Placing a moratorium on new programs for a certain time is a wise move for many churches transitioning into the cell lifestyle. Tell the people that you need to establish the cell philosophy as a way of life in the church.

Compare it to planting a new garden. You give seeds time to grow by rooting out the weeds which destroy new growth, and you must provide sufficient water and sunlight. When you plant the cell church philosophy, you must protect this seedling from the weeds of church programs and competing activities that will eventually choke it out.

No Looking Back

Once the cell groups are established and running, leadership tends to slip back into the program-based mentality. "After all," someone says, "this new program will eventually help the cell ministry." I call these reactions "programmatic knee jerks." Get ready for them. They might not appear for years, but they will surface.

Very subtly, someone in the church desires to add a new evangelism program, para-church organization, social program, and the list goes on-and-on. While none of these are bad, they become problematic when they draw attention and resources from the main thing, cell church ministry.

For example, one church in Chile adopted Marriage Encounter with great effectiveness and became that program's model for Latin America. My mission organization decided to send various national pastors to Chile so they could master this model and implement it in their churches. The mission offered to send our pastor; I objected. Not that I have anything against the program. In fact, God transformed my wife and me at a Marriage Encounter in 1989. I objected because of the simple principle of concentration.

We as a church had not learned to do "one thing" well. We were beginning our cell church transition and once again faced the danger of adding an activity without realizing its drain on our cell system. Resources stretch only so far, so be vigilant and concentrate on this one thing. Ask these questions: Will the new program or activity directly benefit cell ministry or drain precious resources? Can it be accomplished in and through the cell church philosophy? If either answer is no, then say "no."

INTEGRATE EVERYTHING

The battle over the Internet browsers is a hot topic. Some believe that the Microsoft Corporation violated the law by bundling its Internet Explorer browser with its Windows operating system. The U.S. Justice Department charged that the Internet browser was a distinct program and thus needed to be sold separately. Microsoft, on the other hand, emphatically declared that the two were inseparable and thus should be integrated.

This illustration is instructive for the cell church. The issue is which distinct programs are not part of the cell operating system and which ones are inseparable. This is not always easy to determine.

The men's movement called Promise Keepers is a good example of this. God moved in my life when I attended a three-day PK event in 1997, and I believe in this ministry. But if you're transitioning to the cell church and wondering whether you should add PK to your church, what should you do?

First, pray. Second, ask whether Promise Keepers can be integrated into the cell church philosophy. Is it a separate, stand-alone program or can it be incorporated into the new operating system (the cell church philosophy)? If you can't integrate it, and you realize that it will compete for scarce resources, politely decline to add it. Encourage those interested men to attend the nearby rallies.

Yet, perhaps the PK men's groups would actually strengthen the cell vision. If you realize that these groups have all the cell components — knowing God, fellowship, and outreach, you could instruct future leaders that they must multiply their groups. In order to do this, you must make it clear that these groups are an integrated part of the overall cell philosophy, as opposed to independent groups.

In the first scenario, the PK ministry is a threat to your tender cell system; you'd be in danger of losing your focus. In the second scenario, it fits like a glove.

Any program in your church should come under the scrutiny of these questions: Does it square with the operating system of the church? Is it integrated? Does it mesh with the cell philosophy? Bethany's Hornsby counsels: "Whenever an idea is brought up in staff meeting, or when a church member has an idea to start some kind of ministry, ask them and yourself, "Is this sufficiently related to cell groups?"[3] Does it require leadership that functions outside the cell-group ministry? Does it compete with the cell-group ministry for leaders?

WHO LEADS THE CELL MINISTRY?

Senior pastors commonly promote groups but then delegate operation of the small-group ministry to a staff person. When I started a cell ministry under the senior pastor, my area of responsibility was "cell ministry." Everything to do with cell ministry fell under my authority. Sometimes other pastor's responsibilities meshed with mine, but not all the time.

This approach automatically assigns cell ministry the status of "one program among many." You might object and say, "Our cell ministry is important even though we have a director!" I don't doubt that. When the person in charge of cell ministry is someone other than the senior pastor, it relegates cell ministry to one ministry among many. The senior pastor's direct involvement is one of the key distinctions between a church with cells and a cell church. In the cell church, the senior pastor *is* the cell minister. That's his main job. In a church with cells, the senior pastor often delegates small-group ministry to someone else, much as he would any other ministry.

I'm not saying that a church transitioning to the cell model will instantaneously change all staff positions. Quickly re-engineering everyone's job could cause problems. In fact, if your church is transitioning to the cell model, you might designate a point person to work with the senior pastor for a time. The senior pastor, however, eventually must take full charge of cell ministry; he must not delegate this role to anyone else.

CONCLUSION

The awkwardness I felt over Faith Rouse's comment has long since passed, but my friend's advice lingers. How I wish I'd remember it more often. Recently, I said "yes" to oversee a ministry because I thought that I should. I thought: "After all, it's too late to turn back; I'm obligated." For weeks that decision obscured my focus, caused grief, and cost lots of extra work. Christian leader, you must learn to concentrate on cell ministry. The good that knocks at your door is often the enemy of the best that God has for you. The word "no" is a blessed word. Learn to love it and use it often.

9

BLOW

THE TRUMPET

"Isn't David Cho a bit dogmatic by insisting the senior pastor is the key to cell ministry?" I asked myself. "Yes, the role of the senior pastor is important in cell ministry, but not that important." At that time, I had read Cho's writings, penned over 18 years ago: "The [senior] pastor must be the key person involved. Without the pastor, the system will not hold together. It is a system, and a system must have a control point. The controlling factor in home cell groups is the pastor."[1] Is it really that important?

SENIOR PASTOR MUST LEAD
THE CHARGE

Three reasons stir me now to say "amen" to Cho's advice. First, I initiated a cell ministry that eventually stagnated and sets unwrapped on the dusty shelf of church activity. Second, I visited the largest churches in the world. Third, I've since transitioned a church to the cell-church philosophy.

The cell ministry at El Batán church was my baby. I started and carried it. God used me to take the ministry from five cells in 1992 to 51 in 1994. When I left to plant another church, the cell ministry staggered and eventually fell. You'll notice that I've used "I" and "me." This was the problem — too much of ME. In other words, the senior pastor neither initiated nor sustained the cell vision. He thus was slow to establish cell ministry at the heart of the church. After my departure, that church's small groups returned to the status of waiting their turn in the long line of other high-powered programs. That experience reinforces Cho's assertion that cell ministry stems from the vision and the dreams of the senior pastor and not from someone else.

My paradigm shifted again while analyzing the largest cell churches around the world. Each of these churches had one cell director: the senior pastor. The cell system flowed from his authority, and the people willingly submitted and followed his lead. These senior pastors envisioned thousands of people won to Christ through their cell systems. They learned to concentrate on this "one thing" and jealously guarded their single-minded vision. César Castellanos, the senior pastor of Bogota's ICM, is emphatic about this subject:

> "The cell church vision is exciting. Don't stray from it. A cell church must have one vision. You must have only one vision. Love the cell church vision. Love the cell groups."[2]

Such contagious dreaming ignites hungry hearts. Senior pastors like Castellanos, Larry Stockstill and David Cho demonstrate that the senior pastor is crucial to the long-term success of any church's cell ministry. They are the senior leaders of the cell ministry.

All staff members in these successful cell churches are organized around cell ministry. Cell pastors serve under the senior pastor and have a common focus: cells. Rarely is one pastor, other than the senior pastor, placed over the cell ministry. All pastoral staff is over cell ministry and under the senior pastor. In this crucial arrangement, the senior pastor must fulfill the role of cell minister.

The third and perhaps most influential factor was personally transitioning a church to the cell model. This time, God guided me to approach cell ministry in the right manner and with the right heart. Instead of insisting on the title "cell minister" (which others gladly would have given!), I simply became one of the seven cell directors. Each of us had one voice and one vote. We each possessed equal authority, with the notable exception of *the* cell minister, the senior pastor.

I witnessed firsthand that deep, long-term change resides with the senior pastor. He alone could effectively say "no" to the innumerable activities that confronted us. The congregation looked to him to decipher whether the cell-church philosophy was a passing fad or a permanent fixture in the church. Without his modeling of cell-church values and principles, we surely would have withered.

CHARACTERISTICS OF CELL-CHURCH PASTORS

Probably clear by now is the undisputed fact that the senior pastor is the "cell minister" in the cell church. He sets the direction and leads the charge. In the world's largest churches, the senior pastor personally received and carried the cell-church vision. Yet, these pastors share other characteristics worth noting. They are men of prayer, passionate to reach the lost, visionaries, personally involved in cell ministry, and keen on delegation.

Prayer Burden

All of the senior pastors are men of prayer. They live and breathe a life of prayer, thus modeling for the congregation the importance of prayer. Before David Cho preaches, he spends two to three hours in prayer.[3] The first time I heard him speak, the power of the Holy Spirit flowed soundly through him, and subsequent occasions have been similar. The largest church in the history of Christianity is a praying church because its senior pastor models persistent prayer.[4] Cho often spends all night at Prayer Mountain and, through his example, prayer is the accepted way of life at YFGC.

César Castellanos is another example of a life dedicated to prayer. His congregation knows that he spends large amounts of time in prayer and communion with the Holy Spirit. In those times, he receives his worldwide vision for the church. Several of his key leaders attribute their own success to the vision and inspiration of their pastor.

Passion to Reach the City for Christ

Each of these men went out to conquer a city for Christ, not just to grow a church. Their ultimate church-growth goals included hundreds of thousands of people. These pastors believe that their task to reach a world for Jesus Christ was and remains urgent. They intentionally plan and pursue numerical growth. They do not hesitate to set quantifiable goals for their cell ministry. Yet the single motivation for growth is the state of those souls living without Christ. These pastors don't debate the "numbers game" or attempt to build their own kingdoms. They seek the lost strictly for eternal reasons.

Vision and Dreams

The senior pastors in the largest cell churches enjoy immense authority because they excel in capturing, articulating, and implementing God-given dreams and visions. Members of the largest churches demonstrate great respect for and submission to their pastors because they know these men hear from God. The strength and solidity of the pastoral vision gives the congregations the sense that they are part of a work greater than themselves, and that God Himself has spoken to their pastors. Dale Galloway says:

> No matter who introduces small-group ministry into a church, that ministry will only go as far as the Senior Pastor's vision for it. The people will watch the Senior Pastor to see if small-group ministry is important to him or her, because what's important to the Senior Pastor is important to the people.[5]

The pastors of the two largest cell churches in Latin America openly discuss the importance of dreaming big dreams and freely use David Yonggi Cho as their example. These are Cho's words: "When I look back at my own ministry, God first put visions and dreams into my heart, then those visions and dreams developed faith in my soul. Through that faith, God accomplished great ministries."[6] Cho walks around pregnant with his visions and dreams. But he also teaches his under-shepherds to dream big dreams. Cho asks each cell leaders to capture God's vision for his or her group and then to write that vision on paper. Using those pieces of paper, he then directs the leaders to look at and live in their visions.[7] Cho requests his district pastors to ascend the International Fasting and Prayer Mountain to pray and set growth goals for their districts.[8]

Senior pastors must create the environment for success in the cell church by constantly launching and reiterating the vision. This primarily occurs in ongoing training, but it also should resound in the announcements, the sermon, and the award ceremonies (recognizing cell groups giving birth).

Personal Involvement in Cell Ministry

Effective pastors are intimately immersed in cell ministry. The senior pastor at the Elim Church, for example, visits a different cell group each week. How easy it would be for him to say, "I'm the senior pastor of 130,000 people. I don't have time to visit a cell each week!" Yet he understands that this personal involvement keeps him in touch with the life of the cell church. He also knows that modeling personal involvement for those serving under him is a must.

Despite his demanding schedule, Bethany's Larry Stockstill visits cells, writes the weekly cell lesson, meets weekly with his 12 disciples, leads a homogeneous cell, teaches at the monthly leadership summit, and stays acutely abreast of what's happening in cells by reading reports, totals, and the weekly coordinator's report. Stockstill wisely says, "People will always be interested in what the Senior Pastor is interested in."

I found one exception to this level of personal involvement by the senior pastor. In this one church, the pastor delegated cell ministry to a director and is "available" upon call. I noted at the time, "Something is not quite right about this." Recent figures show that the church's cells have stagnated, remaining at the same number for the last two years.

Delegation

Effective cell-church pastors know how to delegate. They're ranchers, par excellence, who rely on those under them to carry out the work of the ministry. They don't even attempt to pastor all of the sheep. Rather, they concentrate on pastoring those who in turn pastor the flock. David Cho is an excellent example of a rancher. He writes:

> My job is not going around visiting from house to house and winning individual souls. My job is to oversee the Cell System.

I delegate my ministry totally to my associates and to my cell leaders. My job is to mange the training institution, and the training program.[9]

Cho delegates responsibility to his laypeople. He believes in the priesthood of all believers, whether they are men or women. Under his leadership, Yoido has grown to more than 725,000 members and more than 25,000 cell groups.

Many in the United States wonder why the cell-church movement hasn't mushroomed in the U.S. like it has in Korea. Pastor Larry Kreider, founder of DOVE Christian Fellowship International, asked Cho for his insight into this issue. Cho didn't hesitate: "The problem here in America is that pastors are not willing to release their laypeople for ministry."[10] Cho is referring to the hesitancy of pastoral leadership in the U.S. to delegate pastoral authority to their cell leaders and interns.

CONCLUSION

While leading cell seminars, I sometimes encounter zealous laypeople who get so excited about the cell model that they want to convert the entire church to the cell philosophy, regardless of whether the senior pastor agrees. While we can applaud this type of excitement and zeal, we must quickly explain the consequences of moving forward without the senior pastor's leadership. Long-lasting change requires a point man. As Cho says, "… a system must have a control point. The controlling factor in home cell groups is the pastor."[11] Without him not only on board but actually leading the charge, a church's cell ministry will sink. Don't begin your cell-church transition unless your senior pastor is leading the charge.

10

DEVELOP A SYSTEM
OF SUPPORT

Cell churches grow exponentially by providing intimate care for each leader. They rely on a support system offering guidance at every leadership level. Everyone is monitored, pastored and held accountable. In some cell churches, leaders are placed over geographical districts, zones or areas of the city. Others supervise their leaders through homogeneous departments.

Are you wondering which kind of system oversight and support to give your cells? And how this system works practically?

A few words of advice: Don't over-complicate your system of oversight and support. Learn the principles from the best support systems around the world, and then apply the principles to your situation. Don't smother yourself by over-structuring. Learn and apply the KISS principles: Keep It Simple, Stupid![1]

Add to the KISS principle your God-given creativity. Some leaders who lack inventiveness hop from one cell model to the next. Don't fall into that trap. Every church starts at a different place. Are you transitioning? You will need to adapt your cell system with this in mind. Are you planting a new church? Use only enough structure to care for your needs.

NECESSITY OF A SUPPORT SYSTEM

Why not forget a system of oversight and support and just concentrate on the cells? For two reasons:

First, you must take care of your leaders. Put another way: You must minister to your ministers if they're going to continue to minister. Jethro advised Moses to reorganize because his system would eventually "wear the people out" (Ex. 18:18). Moses as a one-man-show couldn't minister to everyone, which meant that some eventually would suffer. Developing a support system will help you care for your leaders over the long haul. Larry Stockstill describes the motivation for his system of support: "Our concern is that every single one of our people is pastored well and that we know who is responsible for them in case of a crisis."[2]

Second, you must watch out for your leaders. Paul urged the Ephesians elders:

> Keep watch over yourselves and all the flock of which the Holy Spirit has made you overseers. Be shepherds of the church of God, which he bought with his own blood. I know that after I leave, savage wolves will come in among you and will not spare the flock. Even from your own number men will arise and distort the truth in order to draw away disciples after them. So be on your guard! Remember that for three years I never stopped warning each of you night and day with tears (Acts 20:28-31).

One of the first questions asked during a cell seminar invariably addresses the "danger" of allowing so many laypeople to minister. What about false doctrine and divisions? Don't brush off this question because it's a real concern for many. But a solid cell system covers this need by providing control and vigilance. Your cell system will protect you, your ministry, and your people.

WHERE TO CARE FOR YOUR PEOPLE

Should you organize your cells geographically or according to natural affinity groups? Geographic divisions characterized the cell church for years, but this is changing. The new wave of cell thinking emphasizes homogeneous groupings. Actually, most care systems use a combination of the two.

The support structure of Bethany World Prayer Center is organized geographically. Yet, Pastor Larry asked his leaders in 1997 to launch homogeneous groups. Within months, more than 400 homogeneous cell groups were formed. Such success might then lead to organizing completely around homogeneous groups, which is how ICM in Bogota does it. Bethany, rather, decided to maintain its geographical distinctions. Among the reasons: Geographical divisions make it easier to disciple newcomers. A geographical system simplifies figuring out under whose leadership newcomers belong. Susan, a first-time visitor in the church, lives between Fourth Street and Seventh Street in the northern part of the city, so she will be under the care of District Pastor Tom, who is in charge of this area.[3]

FCBC combines the efficiency of the geographical district with homogeneous groupings. This church has three large geographical districts as well as distinct homogeneous divisions such as Campus District, Youth Zone, Music Zone, Chinese District and Handicap

District. (See the appendix for more about FCBC's creative cell organization.)

When the Republic Church decided to become a cell church, we already had several family groups located in different parts of the city. How would we distribute these groups among the pastors? We decided to take a map, locate the family groups on it, and place the pastors over each geographical location. Geography gave us a starting point and simplified our work. Since then, we have steadily transitioned to homogeneous categories, including women's cells, children's cells, men's cells, young professional cells, English-speaking cells, and more. Cells within homogeneous categories are free to multiply over the entire city, regardless of geography.

Remember that the structure exists to serve you and not the other way around; therefore, make it as simple as possible. If you have 10 cells and two people on staff, consider dividing your area into two broad sectors, one for each staff member. Again, creativity will serve you well.

The International Charismatic Mission, the fastest-growing cell church in the world, has converted almost completely to homogeneous groupings.[4] They united all of the ministries under major categories:

MEN'S CELLS	WOMEN'S CELLS	COUPLE'S CELLS	YOUNG PEOPLE'S CELLS	JUNIOR'S CELLS	CHILDREN'S CELLS
2,300	4,500	1,200	6,500	3,000	150

If a family wants to attend a cell group at ICM, they would choose the homogeneous category called "couples." Men would attend men's cells, over which Pastor Castellanos personally presides. His wife, Claudia, heads the women's cells.

Again, don't over-complicate your cell structure. If you have four family cells in your church, start with this homogeneous grouping. As you form the youth cells, you'll add another category. Use homogeneous cell groups whenever possible, because people naturally feel more comfortable with their own type. Youth like youth cells; young professionals enjoy young professional cells; women relate better to women, men to men, and families to families.

POPULAR SUPPORT MODELS

The 5x5 Model

This is the "classic" support structure, invented by David Cho, for cell churches around the world. This hierarchical system of leadership, in which everyone submits to a higher authority, is most often called the Jethro Model. It's based on the advice that Jethro gave his son-in-law Moses:

> But select capable men from all the people — men who fear God, trustworthy men who hate dishonest gain — and appoint them as officials over thousands, hundreds, fifties and tens. Have them serve as judges for the people at all times, but have them bring every difficult case to you; the simple cases they can decide themselves. That will make your load lighter, because they will share it with you (Ex. 18:21-22).

The Elim Church in San Salvador, El Salvador, follows this model (see appendix), and the core organization of Bethany World Prayer Center also imitates it. Some other examples of fully developed 5x5 structures in the United States are Cornerstone Church and Ministries in Harrisonburg, VA; Colonial Hills Baptist Church in Southhaven, MS; and Shady Grove Church in Grand Prairie, TX.

Under this system, a supervisor cares for five cell leaders; a zone pastor directs 25 cell leaders; and a district pastor supervises approximately 125 cell leaders. A zone averages about 250 people in 25 cells, and a district numbers about 1,250 people in 125 cells.[5]

Carl George, attempting to popularize this model, gave the Roman numeral name X for a cell leader over 10 people; the name L for a supervisor over five cell groups and 50 people; and D for a higher-level leader over 50 cell groups or 500 people. Avoid these names. They require continual explanation and impersonalize the position. Call him or her a cell leader instead of an X, a supervisor instead of an L, and a director or zone pastor instead of a D. Say what you mean, and you won't have to explain later.

The 5x5 system works within geographical boundaries. You might have a South Zone, an East Zone, etc. In the case of Bethany, cells were formed by ZIP codes. Thus, people are assigned to cells whose members live in the same general area.

As the cells multiply in the 5x5 structure, the geographical organization expands.

- If a church begins with three cells in one zone of the city, and those three multiply to five, a supervisor is appointed over the five cell leaders.
- When those five multiply to 10, another supervisor is added and the zone is divided into two geographical sectors (north and south, for example).
- When the zone grows to five sectors with a supervisor over each sector, a zone pastor is appointed over those five sectors.
- When a church reaches five zones, it will appoint a district pastor.

See how the multiplication of cells continues to expand the 5x5 geographical structure. The Elim Church, for example, started in 1985 with no strict geographical control for the cell groups. As the groups multiplied, Elim added zones and eventually two districts. The natural expansion continued and in 1996 Elim included eight districts complete with zones and sectors. This brings up another important reminder: *Don't expand the structure prematurely. Add layers of structure only when needed.*

As the system enlarges in the 5x5 structure, continually develop higher-level leadership. Ralph Neighbour Jr. wisely says: "As the cells increase, the installation of Zone Supervisors is mandatory. If the ratio of five cells to one Zone Supervisor is not maintained, the lack of mentoring and supervision can cause serious problems."[6] Strong systems produce strong cell leaders and, thus, effective cell groups. All leadership needs care, training, and supervision.

One important benefit of the 5x5 model is that new leadership comes from within the church. Successful cell leaders move into supervisory positions and then into full-time pastoral positions.

The major disadvantages of this model concern the cell-multiplication process. Close bonds among cell members are severed when the group multiplies. The new cell comes under the jurisdiction of the area supervisor, not the original cell leader. One pastor confessed that it is difficult to birth new groups because the new cell leader loses ties with the mother group during multiplication. He believes the original cell leader should supervise the new cell, and so he is changing to the G-12 model (discussed later).

Another disadvantage in the 5x5 geographical model is that the cell can multiply only inside the confines of its geographical area. If a group is ready to give birth and the new leader lives in a different zone, he or she would be forced to come under the supervision of another zone leader. Neighbour says:

> The pure, 5x5 structure does so through geographical cells, which seek to reach those living in a district. The difficulty

with a geographical structure is that people often have no natural contact with their neighbors and eventually run out of *oikos* contacts that can be reached. The 5x5 also requires a severing of working relationships by members when new cells are formed.[7]

The G-12 Structure

ICM's César Castellanos originated this care system based on the model of Jesus and His 12 disciples:

> Jesus went up on a mountainside and called to him those he wanted, and they came to him. He appointed twelve — designating them apostles — that they might be with him and that he might send them out to preach and to have authority to drive out demons (Mark 3:13-15).

The G-12 structure is being developed in the U.S. at Bethany World Prayer Center (Baker, LA), Church of the Nations (Athens, GA) and other places. (Bethany's transition to the G-12 system is included in the appendix.)

In the mid-1980s, ICM's cell groups divided into 20 zones around Bogota. About 1990, three major changes took place. First, the church began to emphasize cell multiplication. Second, the cell grouping changed from geographical to homogeneous. Third, the Lord gave César Castellanos the vision that each cell leader needed to raise up 12 more cell leaders and that the cell system should be based on the way Jesus discipled His 12.[8]

Modeling Christ's example, Castellanos handpicked 12 pastors with whom he continues to meet every week. These 12 have 12 under them, and the process continues down to each member of the church. Each person remains with the 12 under whom he or she began the discipleship process. This relationship might last for years, barring unusual circumstances or permission given for someone to change to a different group of 12.[9]

This model does not observe the titles district pastor, zone pastor and supervisor since it is based on homogeneity rather than geography. A non-geographical network reaches women, men, children, youth, professionals, etc. The principle of pastoral care at every leadership level, however, is still very evident.

In this system, every person is a potential leader and every leader is a potential supervisor. This brings a greater willingness to place each church member in cell leadership. Everyone from the senior pastor to the kitchen worker is commissioned to find 12 disciples, primarily from among the new Christians. Any convert at ICM is a potential disciple.

Suppose that John was converted in my cell group, and that I'm hoping he becomes my disciple. I first would move John through the training process (Encounter Retreat, School of Leadership and Second Encounter Retreat). Then I would encourage John to open his own cell group. After completing the training and opening his own cell group, John would be eligible to become "my disciple." I must actively supervise John through these stages before I can officially call him "one of my 12 disciples."

Yet, I also am part of someone else's G-12. Therefore, cell leaders who have found one or more disciples must attend three weekly meetings (open cell, parent G-12 group, personal G-12 group). When the cell leader finds 12 disciples, he no longer is required to lead an open cell. The leadership cell provides nurture, care and mentoring. The personal cell focuses on edification and evangelism.

Discipleship at ICM is not a static, ingrown activity. A disciple must lead a cell group. Instead of waiting for an entire cell group to naturally give birth, this concept compels cell leaders to actively look for laypeople to lead new cell groups and become disciples in the process. The concept of the 12 is a way to multiply groups more rapidly.

This model has some real pluses. Because the leader who multiplies his or her cell supervises the new group, relationships between cell groups are maintained. This model also requires less hierarchy and can be implemented on a grass-roots level. Multiplication occurs more rapidly and greater potential exists for continual multiplication of cell groups (some have over 1,000).

Points of concern include a greater time commitment, attending multiple groups, and various training events and retreats. This creates a problem for many, especially in the U.S.

The G-12 model also asks each person to find 12 permanent disciples. Some might hesitate to commit to a permanent discipleship group.

The quality control also can falter as cell groups multiply at lower levels. One of Castellanos' 12, Rafael Perez, admits that degeneration takes place within the G-12 model. In other words, the original 12 understand the original vision. The farther away a disciple is from the original discipler, the more degeneration occurs. Remedies abound, but be aware of the problem.

CHOOSING AMONG THE ALTERNATIVES

Don't get lost in the forest of cell support systems. Keep it simple and add structure only when necessary. *Remember the basic principle: quality care for each level of leadership.* Strong systems produce effective cell groups.

Remember also to be creative. The Republic Church, for example, uses a mixture of the 5x5 and the G-12. We began with geographical zones, transitioned toward homogeneous groupings, and are implementing the G-12 principles. Several churches maintain their geographical distinctions while implementing the G-12 model. Study the models thoroughly (more information in the appendix) and apply the principles to your context.

God doesn't want you to copy the Bogota model or the Korean model. He has something special for you in your context. Maybe you'll create the next G-7 Model. If you live in Los Angeles, people might call it the Los Angeles Model! Or the Chicago Model! He's given you the power of creativity and wants you to use it.

ESTABLISH
NEW LEADERS

George Whitefield and John Wesley were contemporaries in seventeenth-century England. Both dedicated themselves to God's work in the same small group (Holy Club) at Oxford University. Both were excellent open-air preachers. Both witnessed thousands of conversions through their ministries. Yet John Wesley left behind a 100,000-member church, while George Whitefield could point to little tangible fruit toward the end of his ministry. The difference? Wesley dedicated himself to training and releasing small-group leaders, while Whitefield busied himself with preaching and doing the work of the ministry. Success in the cell church is clear: *How many leaders have been spotted, trained and deployed?*

NEW OPPORTUNITIES FOR LEADERSHIP

When our church passed through a conflict, Carolyn, one of the cell leaders, abruptly left. Even my pleadings didn't convince her to stay.

As the church began to heal, I was grateful that she had left someone in charge of her group, but I began to doubt even Alicia's longevity. "Will Alicia make it as a leader?" I silently wondered. "She's so shy and unassuming. Will she, like Carolyn, eventually leave?"

Not only did Alicia stay, but, 18 months later, she is one of my best leaders. I constantly hold her up as an illustration of the model cell leader over an exemplary cell group. Her small group rarely has fewer than 15 people, and she has multiplied the group three times. Her "young professionals" group respects her as their leader and gathers most weeks for social activities outside the cell meeting.

Alicia is an exemplary lay minister. As children of the Reformation, we believe that every person is a minister. The Bible teaches that all of us are priests (Rev. 1:6). Paul writes in Ephesians 4:11,12 that the principle role of the pastor is to prepare the people to do the work of ministry, not to *do* all the ministry himself. Pastors often excel in teaching people the Word of God. Infinitely more difficult, however, is releasing people to actually *do* the work of ministry.

Are the responsibilities of ministry in your church reserved exclusively for the church pastors and staff? Or is every person — in deed and not just in word — truly considered a minister?

Cell ministry presents what is perhaps the most excellent opportunity for every person to fulfill their role as ministers. Small-group leaders are enabled to minister, pastor, counsel, visit, evangelize and exercise their leadership. In this way, the leaders fulfill the work of the ministry in a very practical way. I agree with Carl George when he says, "I'm convinced that laypeople take the ministry of small groups so seriously that they would prefer to be in charge of a small group than any other ministry in the church."[1]

SET YOUR GOAL:
EVERYONE IS A POTENTIAL LEADER

Many wonder whether only certain "exceptional" people can successfully lead a cell group. There are two schools of thought here:

- If only particular people can lead small groups, these exceptional people will be invited to attend an extra course just for them and the rest will be put on another training track. This is the norm in most churches.
- If everyone is a potential leader, the church's entire training system will prepare to mobilize all members to eventually lead a cell group.

Successful cell churches practice the second option. True, not everyone in these cell churches *will* lead a group for a variety of reasons. But as soon as a small-group system is injected with the thought that only certain people *can* lead a group, that church is greatly limited. People will feel that they don't have the gifts and personality of "so-and-so." While they probably won't have the same giftings and personality as someone else, research shows that those differences do not affect their success in cell leadership.

My statistical study of over 700 small-group leaders reveals that group multiplication is not linked with the leader's gifts, personality, education and so forth. Rather, their achievements have everything to do with their effort (praying for the group, visiting members, setting goals, and other characteristics outlined in my earlier book, *Home Cell Group Explosion*). Since those aspects of cell leadership that determine one's level of success are controllable, anyone can be a successful cell leader. Shouldn't churches, then, view each member as a potential leader? Stating that each person is a potential Christian leader assures members that the church is willing to nurture and grow them into the people God created them to be.

That's what ICM believes. The declared goal of the International Charismatic Mission is to transform every new convert into a dynamic cell leader. ICM's vision is for people to successfully lead a cell group, not just belong to one. Pastor Castellanos often tells his people, "Our goal is not to recruit cell members, but to train leaders."[2] As soon as a new convert starts attending ICM, he or she is placed on the training path that ends in cell leadership. ICM feels compelled to find, train and release new leadership as quickly and efficiently as possible to keep up with the church's phenomenal conversion growth (with 24,000 cell groups, they are doing a good job).

Bethany World Prayer Center has adopted a similar vision. New converts advance through four levels of training with their eyes on the reward of becoming a cell-group leader. New converts know from Day One how to thrive at Bethany. Because the goal is clear, converts are more likely to persevere through the trials, temptations and extra time commitments associated with joining a church family and learning to become Christ-like.

EQUIPPING PEOPLE FOR MINISTRY

Scripture assures us that the Holy Spirit desires to conform us to the image of Jesus Christ (Rom. 8:29). This is a lifelong process. No training course accomplishes what only the Holy Spirit is capable of doing in our lives. Likewise, Paul tells Timothy to meditate on the inspired, inerrant Word of God in order to be "thoroughly equipped for every good work." This also is a process.

Many churches traditionally lump all church members into a generalized system of education (Bible classes, Sunday School, etc.). The hope is that particular individuals will demonstrate higher levels of interest and eventually become leaders. While the intentions are excellent, far too many people fall through the cracks. There is no easy way to track the progress of those passing through this type of system. A large number of candidates drop out. Getting lost in the educational machinery is a recurring flaw in the "general education" approach to leadership training.

As a more effective alternative, the successful cell churches develop an equipping track. A "track" simply is a clearly defined path of specific training that disciples a new believer in God's truth and prepares him or her to lead a cell group. This indoctrination in the essentials prepares new Christians to live abundant and victorious lives, nurtures them through a maturing process and advances them to cell leadership through intensive leadership training. Many equipping tracks have two layers: the first for new Christians, and the second that focuses strictly on leadership preparation.

Baby Christians need more mature Christians to spell out for them — spoon-feed them — how their worldly values contradict those of God's kingdom. They need direction to sort through their values and priorities and line them up with God's. They must understand the basic teaching of God's Word, how to use their spiritual gifts, wage warfare against the enemy, and receive inner healing for past hurts. Prayer and quiet time with the Lord also must become priorities. A new Christian cannot move on to in-depth leadership training without mastering these basics.

The majority of cell churches begin the training process within the cell. In the TOUCH Outreach Ministries training system, for example, *The Arrival Kit* informs the new believer:

> Your Cell Group will be served by one person who will seek to minister to your needs in a special way. Some day, when you have matured, you may also shepherd others as a Cell Leader.

There will never be more than fifteen in your family cell, and you will soon discover that each member is on a spiritual journey with you.[3]

This reinforces that the new-believer training and cell-group involvement occur simultaneously. The seed concerning cell leadership is also planted early in the process.

In the cell environment, members receive training until they become full participants in the group. Because the cell meeting is a training ground for new leadership, each "leader-in-training" should participate. People learn in the process of doing, by getting involved. For example, Marge can lead the worship, or Jim can present and direct the icebreaker. People also learn best by taking incremental steps; that is, the successful completion of a smaller task gives them confidence to tackle a larger one. Begin by asking the person to do something specific: read Scripture, pray, or organize refreshments. Eventually, the potential leader will facilitate the lesson (Word).

EXAMPLES OF DOABLE EQUIPPING TRACKS

One of the keys to a flourishing equipping track is that it is "doable." This word entails a definite start and finish, and it means here that every person in the church must know exactly what that path is. Doable equipping tracks can be clearly and easily explained. Bethany World Prayer Center and the International Charismatic Mission are two churches with doable equipping tracks.

Bethany depicts its track as a baseball diamond, and getting around all the bases takes approximately eight months. At Bethany World Prayer Center, a new believer entering a cell group receives a sponsor (a cell leader or cell member) who guides that person through the *Christianity 101* booklet. This booklet covers: meaning of salvation, water baptism, disciplines of Christian growth, baptism of the Holy Spirit, cell group ministry, and evangelism. Bethany, like most successful cell churches, has constructed a clear training program for the new believer.

Soon after joining Bethany, the new believer learns how to "hit a home run," or how to go from point A (new convert) to point B (cell leader). The goal for everyone is the same: become a cell leader, as illustrated in the following diagram:[4]

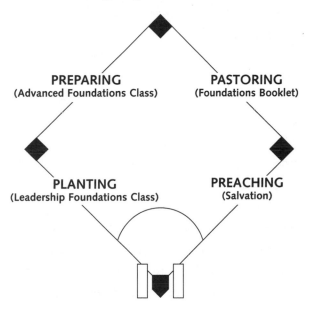

- **First Base:** Water Baptism.
- **Second Base:** Spiritual Formation Retreat. This weekend retreat is designed to deepen the spiritual life of the potential leader. By this time, the potential leader has received discipleship within the cell group.
- **Third Base:** Leadership Formation Retreat, followed by a six-month leadership course.
- **Home Run:** Leading your own cell group. To hit a home run you round first, second and third bases.

The training at the International Charismatic Mission includes:

• **Step One: First Encounter Retreat**
These are spiritual retreats that take place every weekend at designated retreat centers (e.g., ranch home, hotel, farm house, etc.). There is concentrated teaching about liberation from sin, the sanctified life, and the baptism of the Spirit. César Castellanos believes that what can be achieved in one Encounter retreat is worth one whole year of a new believer attending the church.

• **Step Two: First Semester of Leadership School**
The purpose of this three-month training is two-fold: First, to prepare the person in basic Christian doctrine and second, to articulate the vision of ICM.

• **Step Three: Second Encounter Retreat**
This retreat is designed to reinforce the commitments made at the first retreat and to instill final principles in the potential leader before he or she launches a cell group.

• **Step Four: Second and Third Semester of Leadership School**
By the time the student enters the second semester, he or she should be leading a cell group. During these two semesters the disciples are taught more basic doctrine, core values of ICM, and how to deal with false cults.

TOUCH Outreach Ministries explains its equipping system by using a railroad track, and disciples move through the Year of Equipping by advancing through subsequent "stations." With one glance at the track, each potential leader knows the training path. Each resource is organized into daily self-study guides. The first few help cell members realize a new set of values (six months). Members then are introduced to the principles behind relational evangelism and learn to harvest unbelievers who are easy-to-reach, and then those who are more unreceptive to the Gospel.

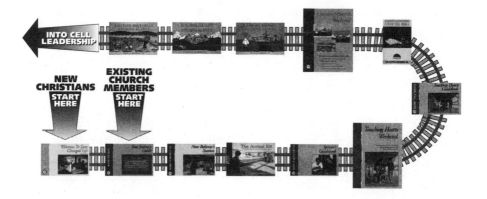

More advanced preparation is necessary before someone actually leads his or her own cell group. ICM offers the intensive School of Leadership discussed above. Bethany's advanced cell leadership training involves a one-day Discovery Retreat, a 12 week Leadership Class, and finally a Champion's Retreat before the person is ordained a cell leader. TOUCH Outreach has developed training for future cell leaders that involves an introductory weekend retreat followed by eight weekly training sessions.

Those who take their cell leadership seriously and continually multiply their cell groups often are elevated to higher positions of leadership (pastors, district leaders, zone leaders, supervisors, cell leaders and administration). This is the pattern in the leading cell churches worldwide. These churches look in their own congregations to fill top leadership positions. Of course, all leaders move through the typical channels of ministerial experience, ministerial success, and leadership training within the church before being lifted up to higher positions.

Provide Service Opportunities

Effective equipping tracks prepare a Christian to live a life of ministry. But the track is not complete unless it offers an effectual outlet for

Christian service. Remember that the principal role of the pastor is to train laypeople to *do* the work of the ministry (Ephesians 4:12). This is where most educational systems fail.

Following is an extreme, but actual, example cited by Carl George. One church in Texas requires each volunteer to take 435 hours of formal classroom instruction before being certified as a layminister. At the end of such training the person can choose among the following ministries: parking lot attendant, greeter-usher, or participant in the seasonal pageant.[5] Granted, most churches present many more ministry possibilities. But do those possibilities allow the new Christian worker to pastor, evangelize, visit, counsel, prepare lessons, and lead other people? Or, again, are these relegated solely to the church staff?

The successful cell churches know nothing of fuzziness and fog in leadership training. The track is clear, and many embark on the doable training for future cell leaders.

CONCLUSION

Successful equipping tracks are clear and doable, and they fit impeccably within the cell structure. The most effective cell churches design their training to relate to the cell structure. It is not a separate department with a different administration. The training system and the cell ministry fit like a glove. The ineffective ones often lose the potential leader through a hazy maze of endless requirements.

Leadership development and training eventually will make or break a cell ministry. While cell multiplication is the principle motivation of cell ministry, the chief goal is leadership development. This is such an important part of the cell church that I'm writing a separate book to fully treat this subject.

FINE-TUNE
THE DETAILS

I'm amazed at the time and care my wife, Celyce, devotes to creating the atmosphere in our home. This was especially noticeable after our last move. She invested days in improving the living room, seeking input on furniture and on the placement of flower arrangements. She spent many hours making ornaments for each wall. Decorating the house is a priority for my wife because it's an extension of her personality, of her character. Celyce believes that physical appearance matters, and she wants visitors to feel warmth and love when they enter our house.

Appearance matters in the cell church as well. What people see when they enter a church building reflects that church's priorities. Some might argue, "We're a spiritual church; the physical appearance doesn't matter." It's true that the life of a cell church is not its physical appearance, organizational chart or budget. But the life of the church is reflected in those things.

For example, God called ancient Israel to physically possess the land to demonstrate their holy calling as God's chosen people. God not only promised that they would be His people, but He also promised to give them a specific land. The identity of God's people centered on God Himself, but it secondarily related to the land of Palestine.

In a similar way, cell churches lay claim to who they are by their physical structure. After all, if cell ministry is important, it will be reflected in the office structure, the organizational chart, the publicity, and the budget. Cell churches are organized with cell at the center of their work and ministry. Cell churches have the opportunity to continually state to those entering their buildings that cell ministry is at the heart of their activities.

Throughout this book, the environment of the home is touted as a key to cell-church effectiveness. But this book is about the cell-church *system*, and successful cell churches possess strong cell systems. They dig deep and lay a lasting foundation, which includes the church building.

OFFICE STRUCTURE

Cell offices make a public, ongoing statement to whoever enters the building that this indeed is a cell church. Without anyone uttering a word, the existence of the offices declares, "We have made a commitment to follow this path. If you want to receive pastoral care here, you'll have to become part of our cell-church philosophy." Physical structures, such as cell offices, reinforce new paradigms as people adapt to change. We know that changes take time, and transitioning to the cell model takes longer than most expect. As people see the physical changes, it will help them grasp the shift of philosophy.

Devoting office space to cells will accomplish little unless the church reorganizes pastoral staff to supervise cell groups. Dynamic cell churches invariably reorganize their pastoral staff, but they don't stop there. Each makes a public proclamation through its cell offices that it is indeed a cell church.

Staff members need adequate facilities to counsel cell members, train new leaders, plan visitation, compile and submit statistics, prepare cell lessons, and make phone calls. Cell offices in the largest cell churches literally buzz with excitement.

Cell-Church Offices

In most of the world's largest cell churches, the office structure declares that small groups form the base of the church. I learned to love those cell churches that physically shaped themselves for the task. These churches maintain an advantage because there is no question about their priorities.

Yoido Full Gospel Church, under Pastor David Cho, pioneered the cell-church office structure. Huge district offices ring the main sanctuary. Maps dotting each district office clearly show the district goals and organization. Desks, one for each subdistrict pastor, form a rectangle around the room, and the district pastor's desk heads the rectangle. Subdistrict pastors sit at their desks on Sundays, ready to counsel needy members or perhaps encourage cell leaders to reach their goals.

The cell offices at Elim Church in San Salvador also form a ring around the main sanctuary. Cell offices are the first visible sight upon entering the church. People seeking counseling visit the district office of their particular geographical area. These district offices are open around the clock on Sundays, and throughout the week.

Faith Community Baptist's cell offices resemble a highly organized enterprise brimming with activity and excitement. Everything has its place. Graphs, charts, and goals explode from every cubicle. Bethany's pastor, Larry Stockstill, compares the Singapore offices to "a military strategy room in the Pentagon." He wondered:

"Why have I never seen a 'District Office' in America? Could this serve as a spiritual 'Command Post' where the invisible cell structure could become visible and cell leaders could find their 'address' in the church?"[1] When you walk into a district office at FCBC, it would look something like this:[2]

TYPICAL DISTRICT OFFICE LAYOUT

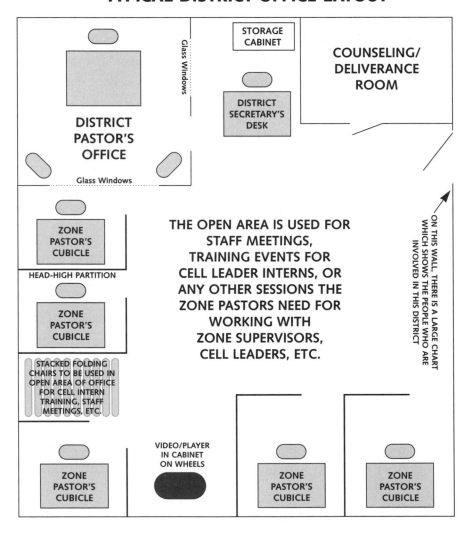

God later worked through Stockstill to establish a command post in North America. Bethany's district offices, called Touch Center, are the strategic hub and nerve center of the church. All vital cell planning, counseling, mapping, and general preparation takes place in those offices, which contain a mailbox for every cell leader. The invisible cell structure has become visible at Bethany.

Where to Start

Those churches just starting their transition to cells may not be ready to build huge offices, and the above examples may seem intimidating. Start by using what you have. Maybe you have one extra office designated for youth ministries. Change it to the cell office. Hang a sign outside the door that indicates the new cell focus:

> ## YOUTH CELLS
> ## DIRECTOR JOHN SMITH

The Republic Church has been transitioning from a church with cells to a cell church since August 1997. One of the first changes was to hire a full-time secretary of cell ministry. We redesigned existing offices with new signs indicating our cell focus. We hung large maps on each office wall, pinpointing the cells under each homogeneous area. We posted pictures of our cell leaders, as well as the time and place of their cell meetings. Again, the physical changes planted a flag in the church. It said, "We are a cell church. Get used to it."

PUBLICITY

When transitioning to a cell church, pay attention to details. Little things often determine success or failure. The details position the cell-church philosophy before the church members and the community-at-large.

"Don't keep on talking about cell ministry," one pastor said. "The people will get tired of it." Don't believe these arguments or allow such negativism to influence your commitment to proclaim, publicize, and market the cell-church philosophy.

Those who understand the place of vision in the church state that a church can't proclaim its vision enough. Repeat it at every opportunity. I agree with George Barna when he writes in *The Power of Vision*: "Those leaders who have been most successful contend that you must take advantage of all opportunities, at all times, to share the vision."[3] Our vision statement at the Republic Church is: "*Quito al Encuentro con Dios a través de una Iglesia Celular*" (that Quito would have an encounter with God through a cell church). We declare this truth at every opportunity.

THE BULLETIN

The typical church bulletin has a place for everything. Jody's bake sale receives prime space, and the men's special outing is pasted on the inside cover. It probably lacks a theme and boils down to a hodgepodge of activity scattered throughout the pages. Who even decides which announcements receive top priority? Usually the church secretary, or perhaps the senior pastor plays an important role.

In many churches with groups, the cell ministry is one program among many. Something about cells might appear each week, but a plethora of programs always appear alongside. The congregation receives the message that attending a cell group is one option, but certainly not the most important. One Sunday, the latest evangelism program might get full attention; the next Sunday, the women's ministry vies for the central place.

Bulletins in cell churches should be different. The bulletin holds a central place in freezing cell-church changes. When a visitor sees the cell-church vision reflected in the bulletin, it doesn't take long to capture the heartbeat of the church.

At the Republic Church, for example, we dedicate the entire inside portion of the bulletin to cell ministry. We highlight one homogeneous cell zone each week. Every eighth week, we show the entire organizational chart, so people see the big picture and the new cells. All cell announcements appear on the inside cover; all other announcements are found on the back of the bulletin.

THE ANNOUNCEMENTS

Most churches make time for announcements, either before the preaching or at the end of the service. If cell ministry is a priority in your church, this should be reflected in the announcements.

At the Republic Church, with over 120 cell groups, cell ministry is the primary activity. Therefore it should be the primary announcement. One of the seven directors, on a rotating basis, presents his area each week. If a cell member was healed, she can share it with the entire church. We also present the new groups that will open during the next week. Cell ministry presence is constantly highlighted, and the entire congregation begins to perceive that all pastoring, counseling, training, and discipleship happens through cell ministry.

Those attending the Sunday celebration need to realize that pastoral care and ministry is offered through the cell system. They must start attending a cell group to tap into those resources.

Banners and Wall Hangings

On the wall behind ICM's pulpit hangs a gigantic banner declaring how many new cells ICM plans to launch by the end of the year. The goal isn't church membership, baptism, or even attendance. The goal is how many cell groups! An even larger banner hangs from the wall at the Living Water Church. This banner proclaims, "Cell Ministry: Our Method of Reaching Peru with the Gospel." Banners at the Christian Center in Guayaquil, Ecuador, make similar statements. The banners, wall hangings, and bulletin boards in these churches declare the cell philosophy to newcomers and remind the faithful of the primary focus.

Bulletin boards can hold pictures of the latest cell retreat, the latest statistics and graphs of the cell-group growth, or the leadership training system. Do the same with cell maps. Republic Church constructed a large map locating all of our cells throughout the city, and placed it at the entryway of the church. When the sanctuary was enlarged, that map moved to the front so the entire congregation would see it throughout the service. Some objected: "It's not practical there because people won't naturally approach it in front." They were right, but they missed the larger point. This huge cell map announced throughout the service: "We are a cell church." To the newcomer it announced: "Join a cell group."

The cell church is a growing, expanding church. New people and traditionalists must understand that cell ministry is central in the church. Some call these tactics "marketing," but it's just common sense. Because of the difficulty of transitioning a church from the traditional model to the cell model, remind people of the cell focus by constantly placing cells in front of them.

ORGANIZATIONAL CHART

An organization chart says a lot about a church's priorities. While transitioning to the cell-church philosophy, carefully form an organizational chart. Is cell ministry at the center of ministry? Can everyone see that in the organizational chart?

One of the most innovative cell churches that I studied had an organizational chart that betrayed its cell ministry focus. Cells were the base of this church, and no one could join another ministry or be a member without active involvement in a cell. But on the organizational chart, cells were sidelined to one ministry among many. Five or six additional categories appeared on the same level as cell ministry.

These other ministries were important, but they were considered separate programs on the chart instead of feeding the cell ministry. In reality, all the other ministries served the cell ministry. The head pastor topped the organizational chart, the two co-pastors were underneath, and the various directors of counseling, worship, children's ministry, and cells were on the same level underneath these pastors. Their organizational chart was confusing because it didn't reflect cell ministry as the church's base:

Before making an organizational chart, ask these questions:
- Are small groups just one of many ministries?
- Do staff members have departmental ministries apart from cells?
- Does the senior pastor lead the cell ministry?
- What is the connection of additional ministries to the cell structure (children's ministry, counseling, etc.)

The important question is: *How does everything else on the chart relate to cell ministry?*

Cell categories (geographical or homogeneous areas) should appear directly under the senior pastor. The organizational chart also should clearly demonstrate that nothing competes with the cell-based structure.

This organizational chart at the Republic Church appears in the bulletin every two months:

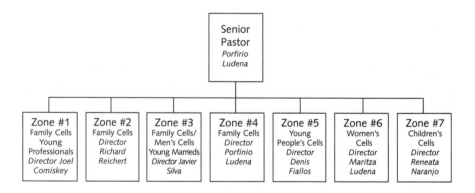

To be honest, I'm not satisfied with the word "zone." We're organized homogeneously as opposed to geographically.[4] Geography only helped us initially to decide under which director we'd place the existing cells. But the above organizational chart does clarify the centrality of cell ministry.

BUDGETING FOR THE CELL CHURCH

"Put your money where your mouth is." This well-worn saying applies to the cell church. The church budget should reflect that it's either a cell church or a church transitioning to cells. What would such a budget include? Following is the budget that I proposed for my zone in 1998:

1998 BUDGET FOR JOEL COMISKEY'S ZONE

OFFICE MATERIALS
  1. Books for the cell library: $500.00
  2. Cell accessories: $550.00
       a. Signs
       b. Maps
       c. Banners
       d. Bulletin Boards
       e. Gifts to recognize successful cell leaders
  3. Copies of cell lessons and other cell materials for cell leaders: $100.00

CELL EDUCATION
  1. Trips to the cell conference Guayaquil (The Christian Center)
       a. Leaders: Scholarship for these conferences: $100.00
       b. Leaders: Trips to other cell conferences for special training: $100.00
  2. Two trips to the International Charismatic Mission: $450.00
       a. One trip with the senior pastor
       b. One trip with the pastor of cells for young people
  3. Retreats: $50.00
       a. For new cell leaders (two before November 1998)
       b. For new members (three before November 1998)

SPECIAL EVENTS FOR ALL CELL LEADERS
  1. Cell leader dinner in December
  2. Retreat for the entire church

Surely, anyone could devise a more professional budget. This budget reflects the economy of Ecuador and the size of my zone. The cell takes priority in our church and this is reflected in how we spend our money. Your budget reflects your priorities.

People spend money on what's important to them. If your church board, for example, balks at spending money on cell ministry, it reflects the board members' true priority. This happened during the early days at the Republic Church, when money for basic cell considerations was hard to find. I talked directly to the administrator and to certain board members: "If we're a cell church, there shouldn't be any hesitancy to spend money on these items. Where we spend our money should reflect our priorities." The administrator since has become one of the church members most convinced of the cell-church philosophy.

OFFERINGS TAKEN IN THE CELL MEETING

Many cell churches take offerings in the cell group. In fact, six of the eight cell churches in my study take offerings every cell meeting.[5] These offerings are turned in to the central administration of the church, though in some cases the cells are allowed to spend some of the money.

For these six cell churches, taking offerings in the cell meeting gives the group a sense of responsibility. Treasurers in each cell faithfully take the money to the church Sunday mornings. At Elim Church, the orderliness and first-class organization of collecting the offerings is amazing. Each leader brings the offering taken in the cell meeting and drops it in a designated slot. Trained staff members count the thousands of envelopes throughout the day.

These cells don't plead for money. Rather, the cell offering is a vehicle to connect the cell with the celebration. These cells aren't isolated units or house churches. Week after week, the cell members also attend the celebration service, and the offering to the mother church reflects that commitment.

At least 65 percent of members in most cell churches attend both cell and celebration. Yet, some who attend the cell are not yet committed to the celebration, and some who attend the celebration still do not attend the cell. Many cell churches believe that those in a cell who have not yet committed to the celebration service should have the opportunity to contribute to the church. After all, they're benefiting directly from the cell group. The cell group is church for some who still have not accepted the celebration as theirs.

Not every cell church takes offerings within the cell. Bethany World Prayer Center, in fact, forbids financial dealings in the cells, apart from an occasional love offering.[6] Each church needs to decide according to its own needs and context.

CHILDREN'S MINISTRY IN THE CELL CHURCH

What do cell churches do with children on Sundays? Some mistakenly think that the cell church overlooks children. Actually, there is no excuse for "half-baked" children's ministry in the cell church. Children are important to God, and all followers of Jesus must prioritize children.

> Jesus said to His disciples: 'Who is the greatest in the kingdom of heaven?' He called a little child and had him stand among them. And he said: 'I tell you the truth, unless you change and become like little children, you will never enter the kingdom of heaven. Therefore, whoever humbles himself like this child is the greatest in the kingdom of heaven' (Matthew 18:1-4).

A cell church must offer a first-class Sunday celebration service (while dividing into smaller groups as well) for kids, as well as provide the cell atmosphere during the week. This dual emphasis adds vitality to the children's ministry.

Children in the Celebration

Children's ministry on Sunday morning is vital. It might not be called Sunday School, but it's the same idea. Adults celebrate every Sunday in a large gathering. Shouldn't the children? Adults hear the Word of God preached in the sanctuary. Shouldn't the children? Yes, God calls children to celebrate and to learn on Sundays.

Often, cell churches call their equivalent of Sunday School "Children's Celebration." The children meet for corporate worship and later divide into age-relevant classes to learn a biblical lesson. Pastor Larry Stockstill of Bethany World Prayer Center says, "… it's important to have a children's celebration. Kids enjoy that same dynamic when they get together."[7] Bethany World Prayer Center teaches the children a Bible theme on Sunday morning and then uses that theme in the home cell groups for children during the week.

Some cell churches, such as Elim Church, find all their Sunday School teachers through the various districts on a rotating basis. The district pastor locates from the cell groups enough qualified teachers willing to lead Children's Celebration. Many churches follow this example, proving once again that a church's needs can be met through the cell system.

Children in Cells

Faith Community Baptist Church is an outstanding model of cell ministry to children. In "intergenerational cells," children and adults gather in the regular cell meeting for the icebreaker and worship. Children quickly add new life to a routine cell meeting! After worship, the children are dismissed for a separate lesson time. While the adults interact with God's Word based on the weekly sermon, the children follow material related to their Sunday celebration experience. It's first-class.

Elim Church in San Salvador ministers to more than 60,000 children every week. Unlike the intergenerational cells at FCBC, children's cells at Elim meet independently. They take place during the adult cells, but in another room of the house. One member of the adult cell leadership team usually senses a call to lead the children's cell group. If not, each adult on the cell leadership team rotates teaching the children.

Most children's cells are counted as "normal" cell groups. What's a normal children's cell group? It includes worship, sharing, Bible memory, Bible lesson (well-illustrated), and refreshments. Like in the adult groups, participation is promoted in these groups. Bethany World Prayer Center often uses videos in children's cells. Children's cell groups, like their adult counterparts, emphasize both evangelization and edification.

CONCLUSION

Remember that details matter as a church transitions into cells. Fine-tuning a church for growth means paying attention to the church building's physical structure and appearance. Powerful cell systems feed healthy cells, not the other way around. To start well and have an ample chance of success, think and pray seriously about how cell ministry is presented to the rest of the church.

EXCEL IN

CELEBRATION

"Let's hurry or we won't find a seat," Jimmy said on our way to the modern indoor stadium in Singapore. Jimmy and I had met the night before in a cell group of Faith Community Baptist Church.

"Everything is professional and well-organized," I thought, as the ushers guided us to the second and third levels of the 10,000-seat stadium. After noticing those around us, I asked Jimmy, "Is it normal to have so many young people in the celebration service?" "Uh huh, about 65 percent of our congregation is 30 or under."

No one had to announce that the service was starting. Forty members of the worship team marched from the curtains to the stadium floor, waving colorful banners in synchronized motions. Then they began to dance and leap across the floor, as two worship leaders guided the congregation. All wore beautiful, matching clothes as they led us in energetic praise to God.

The worship leaders alternated between Chinese and English. Because of our distance from the stage, I couldn't immediately distinguish who was actually leading the worship. I noticed that one of the two worship leaders was in constant motion. Suddenly, it dawned on me that the "lively one" was none other than Lawrence Khong, the senior pastor!

"Top quality" is how I would evaluate the worship at FCBC. Everything in that service was done with excellence. The preaching was clear, biblically based, and relevant. Pastor Khong even translated the entire message from English to Chinese, and I wasn't a bit bored. Many worldwide know FCBC because of its powerful cell system. But FCBC offers a weekly celebration service that is truly exemplary and just as powerful as its cells.

THREE CHARACTERISTICS OF EFFECTIVE CELEBRATION

Successful cell churches share similar patterns in their celebration services. Culling the so-called top characteristics from the abundance of possibilities — the opportunity to receive ministry, the experience of the Holy Spirit, cultural relevancy, etc. — obviously requires subjectivity. But I pick these three characteristics: inspiring, well-planned, and powerful preaching.

Inspiring: Synonyms include stimulating, exhilarating, exciting, refreshing, and invigorating. "Fun" may even be appropriate. Christian Schwarz writes, "People attending truly 'inspired' services typically indicate that 'going to church is fun.'"[1] We're talking here about excitement that comes from the filling of the Holy Spirit and complete dependence on Him. During one cell-church worship service, I wrote, "Here is life! This is Your sovereign work! This is a clean, dynamic expression of God's love.

The shouts of joy spread like wildfire across the auditorium. This is not just wild, charismatic individualism. There is order everywhere." I agree with the observation of Christian Schwarz. Worship should be fun!

Well-Planned: The Holy Spirit makes a service exciting, but He expects diligent planning from us. The inspired spontaneity that reigns in these services results from hours of planning. Take one worship team, for example. Thirteen musicians on stage, all immaculately dressed with matching clothes, play their instruments in perfect timing, and even sway in unison to the beat. Everything looks so easy, but hours of sacrificial preparation go into these excellent worship services. The phrase "well-planned" doesn't exclusively refer to the worship but also to the ushers, greeters, announcements, special music, and the general atmosphere.

Powerful Preaching: Top-notch, Spirit-filled preaching is the norm in these cell churches. After hearing the Word, church members depart satisfied. They receive a first-class sermon, and the pastor applies the Word of God to practical issues. The senior pastor accepts the major responsibility to preach the Word. The sheer size of a few of these churches compels the senior pastor to sometimes share this responsibility.

CELEBRATION STRENGTHENS CELL MINISTRY

When we talk about the cell church, we're referring to both cell and celebration. The cell church is a celebrating church. The cell is not more important than the celebration, nor is the celebration more important than the cell. Both hold equal weight. The goal of the cell leader is not only to grow his cell group, but also to assure that all cell members attend the celebration service on Sunday morning, thus becoming an integral part of the church.

Notice how cell and celebration compliment each other:

1. The cell provides intimacy and accountability. The celebration extols the greatness of God as all of His people worship together.
2. The cell includes personal, individual shepherding. The celebration highlights higher-level leadership.[2]
3. The cell emphasizes the application of the Word of God. The celebration service includes the teaching of God's Word and often the sacraments.[3] Each leader attempts to bring all cell members to the celebration to hear the Word preached and to participate in the sacraments.

Successful cell churches around the world intricately link cell ministry to the celebration service. Great care is taken to guarantee that individual cells share the same vision and philosophy as the mother church, of which they are an extension.

To assure this continuity, cell churches provide cell lessons based on the senior pastor's message. Although each church uses a different style or format for creating the lesson, without exception, the pastor's message is always the foundation. Cell leaders are facilitators — not official pastors. Most do not have formal theological training. Their primary job is to facilitate the group discussion and to pastor those in the group. Providing the cell lessons helps to maintain doctrinal purity, relieve pressure from the cell leader, and assure that young Christians can also lead a cell group. This way, cell leaders can concentrate on their responsibilities, and the tie between the cell and the celebration is strengthened.

Celebration at YFGC

The celebration service at Yoido Full Gospel Church is a stunning combination of fervor, traditional hymns, fully dressed choirs and sound preaching. Each service features a different choir in bright, matching robes. A conductor leads both the orchestra and the choir.

The worship service is user-friendly, high-tech, and extremely well-organized. In each service in the main sanctuary, over 12,000 people are served communion in a matter of minutes. The wine and rice cakes (for bread) are passed simultaneously down the pews. Members sip the wine with communion trays in hand, thus making it easier to immediately return the empty cup.

Cho's preaching is soundly biblical. The day I visited, he repeatedly called the church to repentance, specifically rebuking superficiality in the congregation. Cho boldly spoke against corruption in the Korean government, even to the point of naming the Korean president and a current scandal. Concerning Cho's preaching, I wrote, "Cho is one of the best preachers that I know. He gave a very clear illustration of the political corruption in Korea. He goes from the Word to illustrations. His preaching is big. He talked about Achan being in Korea."

YFGC prays together simultaneously during celebration services. What a joy to finally hear so many voices raised in one accord to the throne of God! Diligent prayers (often spoken in tongues) ascend to the throne in unison. When a bell rings, silence fills the room.

The early worship services cater to the adult population at YFGC. The afternoon worship services minister to the young people. The ushers and choirs in the afternoon come from the youth as well.

Workers at YFGC are clearly distinguishable. Women ushers dress in bright blue and white Korean dresses. Elders who serve communion wear white gloves while serving. All male workers wear white coats. All of them wear badges, distinguishing their role.

YFGC has perfected the use of closed-circuit TV. The service is projected on a huge screen on the main floor of the sanctuary. Photos of the congregation, clips of Cho's current crusade (when he's away), Scripture readings, and words of hymns are all shown on the large screen. These pictures are transmitted simultaneously to hundreds of TV screens throughout the complex. Some services (especially when Cho preaches) are transmitted live to the various chapels throughout the church. At other times, one of the 700 pastors might preach at the separate chapels, while another pastor is preaching in the main sanctuary. At all times, a staff pastor is in charge in each chapel.

BUT I'M A SMALLER CHURCH ...

The average-sized church in North America is between 50 and 75 people. I know the struggle of pastoring a small church; I've been there. It's hard to celebrate when so many seats are empty. And, yes, a large congregation helps provide a dynamic, festive celebration. But there is something more important. The largest churches in the world started with one dynamic: excellence. If churches excel with what that have, God will give them more. Concentrate on the phrase "top-quality." God is not asking any other church to be like YFGC. He's asking all churches to do their best in their particular situation.

Here are a few pointers. First, invite Jesus through prayer to make each worship service exciting and dynamic. Second, plan the celebration service in detail, from the ushers to the music. Third, prepare the sermon as if preaching to 5,000. God will do the rest. He will bring the harvest.

HARVESTING THROUGH CELEBRATION

Some presume that the cell church celebration service focuses entirely on believers. "Cells evangelize and the celebration edifies" is the thinking of many. Yet, the largest cell churches in the world escape such classification by reaping the harvest both within the cell and in the celebration service.

Pastor César Castellanos of ICM does everything possible to make the Sunday worship services palatable to non-Christians. Hundreds go forward each week after he gives the invitation to receive Christ. They immediately are integrated into the cell system.

Elim Church gives salvation messages in its six worship services, and about 50 people receive the Lord in each service.[4] At Bethany World Prayer Center, Pastor Larry invites people to receive Jesus in nearly every service. The cell system is ready to conserve the fruit.

FCBC uses annual "harvest events" to evangelize the lost. In December, they stage an evangelistic event called "Come Celebrate Christmas." In August, they hold a large music concert to reap the harvest. Thousands receive Jesus every year through these events.

In most cell churches, the majority of conversions happen at the cell level. A mighty harvest occurs as cells focus on multiplication through conversion growth. But cell churches are not limited to cell-group conversion. The celebration service also offers exciting opportunities to reap the harvest.

CONCLUSION

Cell churches thrive when an intricate balance exists between the cells and the celebration. Some churches over-emphasize the cell to the neglect of the celebration, or the celebration to the neglect of the cell. Yet, both are essential.

Flourishing cell churches throughout the world excel in both cell and celebration. Their cells are life-giving and reproducing. Their celebration services are inspiring, well-planned, and feature powerful preaching. When quality cells combine with a dynamic celebration, a spiritual explosion occurs that's capable of unstoppable church growth. That's the dynamic in the largest churches in the world.

14

PREPARE FOR THE
TRANSITION

Have you ever placed a new coat of paint on rotting wood? Instead of permanently correcting the problem by cutting out the decay, many opt for the short-term fix. And it works ... for a little while. Then strips of paint start peeling and splotches of bare wood peek through the once pristine exterior.

Small-group ministry in many churches is like a coat of new paint applied over rotting wood. Loads of excitement accompanies the start. "We finally have small groups in our church," excited members proclaim. But then the faulty infrastructure kicks in, reducing the small groups to independent, roaming Bible studies. I have dealt with these autonomous groups after two years of rotating in their own solar system. I even pleaded with them to join our cell system. "Well, we have our own way of looking at small groups," the leader politely replied.

At some point, the rotting wood must be replaced. The key: think long-term. A quick-fix, small-group solution may feel great at the time. It may solve the problem — or drive it underground — for two, three, or four years. But it will surface again — and in greater force — possibly with another pastor in the chair. While it's feasible to experience some short-term success this way, it is nearly impossible to build a ministry that will endure for the long-term. More often, a false start leads to a church that says, "We tried small groups once, and they didn't work."

We prepare for those things we value. When we don't prepare for something, it's because we don't value it. Preparing to make cell ministry work in your church will take loads of energy and time.

THE PROCESS OF CHANGE

"I'm sure that they'll accept our proposal," I thought. After all, we as the pastors of this church had decided to convert the church into a cell church. Then the meeting began. Two hours later, bruised and battered, I wondered what went wrong. That night it became crystal clear to me that the church wasn't interested in our plans for change: The cell ministry would remain one program among many. I learned that evening that tradition is deep-rooted and doesn't budge easily.

Shelves of books have been written about the dynamics of change. Anyone attempting to transition a church to the cell-church philosophy would do well to understand the dynamics of change in the process of becoming a cell church. Managing the dynamics of change is one of the critical issues involved with starting or rebuilding a small-groups ministry in a congregation. If the changes are handled well, the introduction of small groups can be a real blessing.

Remember this: Anytime something new is introduced into the life of a church, a potential for conflict exists. Introducing a new small-group ministry always involves change.

Change Takes Time

Give yourself time, and keep in mind this well-worn adage: "Everything takes longer than you expect, even when you expect it to take longer than you expect." It takes longer to build a skyscraper than a woodshed. The difference lies in the foundation. The depth of your dig depends on the size and the purpose of your building.

People need time to process their ideas about the cell church, just as it took you time to reach conclusions. Their heads will enthusiastically nod as you introduce the concept of these new small groups, but they still need time to digest the implications. Different people respond to change at different rates, and the time involved is not necessarily based on their spiritual maturity.

This leads to another question: How long do you plan on staying in your present ministry? After introducing the changes, do you plan on seeing them take hold? Don't even start unless you're willing to see the transition to completion. This might take five years and, at some point, every pastor wants to bail out and find greener pastures. Just when you think you're making progress, all hell will break lose. I call these moments "programmatic knee jerks." Count the cost and hang-in for the whole ride.

Don't Force Change

When Dr. Bobby Clinton teaches the "Change Dynamics" class at Fuller Theological Seminary, he recites this one-liner: "A person convinced against his will is of the same opinion still." Overlooking the wisdom of this phrase could haunt you later.

I now live in Ecuador with the results of forced change that haunt the Roman Catholic Church. When the Spanish invaded the land 500 years ago, the Indians were given the choice of conversion or death.

Naturally, they converted. Although these indigenous people officially became Catholics, they simply changed the names of their personal deities to the saints of the Catholic religion. The conquerors destroyed the ancient temples and built their churches on the same spots. To this day, these spots remain sacred to the indigenous people. They are in the church physically, but not emotionally or spiritually. Records indicate that the whole country converted to Catholicism 500 years ago. Yet the present state of the indigenous people proves the truthfulness of the statement: "A person convinced against his will is of the same opinion still."

Don't try to immediately convert your people against their will. Prepare them well and then get ready for the long process of change.

CHANGE IS A COMPLEX PROCESS

Churches are composed of countless and often invisible interactions among people, beliefs, and external forces. The implications of these components upon one another may take years to fully play out. The linkage between cause and effect is not always obvious.

People desire to maintain the status quo because it helps them feel settled. Lyle Schaller says, "Every organization tends to move in the direction of redefining purpose in terms of institutional maintenance and survival. ... The care and feeding of the organization, rather than service to the clientele."[1] Once an organization or system gets in motion, it tends to keep going in the same way. People become comfortable with their traditions and patterns and keep doing things in the same way.

Four Key Steps to Change

Step One: Create the Need for Change

Most people receive Jesus Christ as their Savior during a time of crisis. Circumstances create a need, and the person is open to the Gospel. This is the context for change: need, turmoil, desperation. Unless there is a need for change, people will resist it. They are content with the status quo.

Is there a need for change in your church? Some people are content with the status quo. They refuse to change because they don't see the need or perhaps just overlook it. "I want my same group of friends and my same circle of influence," they express unconsciously. This is normal.

Many churches languish year after year in the same desperate state of stagnation. They limp along because certain people diligently guard the gate called change. They steadfastly refuse to allow any changes to upset the status quo. It's like heating up a frog in a pan. The frog doesn't realize the turmoil until it's too late.

Experts tell us that people need to be discontent with the present situation before any intentional, internally motivated, and directed change can occur. The change agent is concerned with this question, "Is anyone else dissatisfied with the present situation?"[2]

Bobby Clinton says, "Often a first task of the agent of change is to increase discontent in order to open the door for intentional change. This sometimes strikes a Christian leader as unethical at first glance. But careful analysis shows that this technique is basically what is done when an evangelist preaches so as to convict sinners of their need for God's salvation."[3]

The proven way to increase discontent is when God's Holy Spirit reveals the need to return to New Testament norms — community, servanthood, the priesthood of all believers, to name a few. This might come through the preaching of the Word or in deep times of prayer.

Another approach is to thoroughly analyze your church's growth patterns, areas of strengths and weaknesses, and future projections. The 40-page analysis that the Republic Church accomplished in September 1997 created the need for change. It unearthed the inherent weakness of our "Sunday morning only" church ministry. We realized that our structures weren't biblical. Agitated by what we saw, we felt drawn to the cell-church approach. Instead of showing your congregation just the future vision, explain which poor decisions led to the church's present state. This will give your people a reason to follow the change process.

Step Two: Make the Changes

Once you've created the need for change, act quickly. You have a window of opportunity, but it won't last forever. When I returned to the Republic Church, God had opened the door for change. The first thing the cell director told me was, "We really need help." One door after another opened, but we had to act.

Step Three: Prepare for the Reaction

After making the changes, get ready to fight the mixed reactions. Everyone likes something new — for a little while. But when push comes to shove, the tendency is to reach for the old, the established, the traditional. This is human nature.

During these "programmatic knee jerks," people begin to realize that the change will affect them in the practical details of their daily living. They grasp that the change might affect the structure of Sunday School or the church's ability to accept all and every program. Some will holler one thing; others will yell another. This is when it gets tough, and you just have to hang on for dear life until the changes are frozen, meaning until everyone is on board.

As you start your cell ministry, it's young and tender. Focus on it rather than on redirecting energies to accommodate the latest fad. This is what we did at Republic Church, over and over again. I wrote the following to one fellow missionary:

> I'm suggesting that we place a moratorium on new programs for 14 months in our church. By God's grace, in 14 months we will have over 100 cells and will have begun to establish the cell philosophy as a way of life in our church. If at that time we notice weak areas in our church that require additional programs, we could more readily integrate them with our cell philosophy. Since arriving in Ecuador, I personally have had to fight off a multitude of well-intentioned programs: a new School, a Jr. High program apart from cells, a welfare program, Promise Keepers, Evangelism Explosion, Marriage Encounter program, and more. The pressure to add programs has come from without and from within. I suppose that instead of decreasing, these petitions and plans will increase.

Expect the established system to push back. Some people who pat you on the back during the initial stages will suddenly recoil when you stop promoting their pet program. TOUCH Outreach Ministries' training material offers valuable advice: "Welcome the initial opposition. Resistance is a good sign. It means people understand what you are saying and are grappling with it!"[4]

Sometimes resistance does not come from one person but from the traditional church culture as a whole, which doesn't know how to handle the change. Church members often deal with their pent-up fears by spreading their discontent through gossip, and you most likely won't know that it's occurring. Hang tight. Most agents of change who give up often do so just before a breakthrough to success.[5]

Step Four: Freeze the Changes

"You must freeze the changes for long-term results." This is the phrase that I remember most vividly from Bobby Clinton's "Change Dynamics" class. Missionaries, for example, often implement programs that are dropped by the nationals as soon as they leave the field. The changes don't stabilize and become a part of the natural system. If there's no missionary to push the program, there's no program. The stabilization of a change into a system is crucial.[6]

After the initial excitement settles down, some church members will long for the "former things." These same people might have agreed with the changes in the beginning but perhaps didn't understand all the implications. They begin to yearn for the "way things were."

Expect this to happen, because it invariably will. And don't give up. Changes eventually will lock into the system and become habit. Therefore, guarding those changes until they become part of the church culture is essential. Those who initially resisted you will begin to support you. The changes will become a way of life for you and your church. You'll perceive permanent change when the leadership takes ownership for the innovation and are overseeing its implementation.

CONCLUSION

In the early days of long sea voyages, scurvy (a disease which resulted from a deficiency of vitamin C) killed more sailors than warfare, accidents, and all other causes of death. In 1601, Captain James Lancaster of the British navy conducted an experiment to evaluate the effectiveness of lemon juice in preventing scurvy on four ships. He gave daily portions of lemon juice to the men on one ship, while the men aboard the other three ships received nothing. Those receiving the lemon juice remained healthy; 110 of the 278 men on the other three ships died of scurvy.

The results were so clear that the entire British navy immediately adopted the new cure, right? Sadly, "citrus juice" wasn't adopted as the official cure for scurvy in the British marines until 1795 (194 years later). Part of the resistance stemmed from competing remedies offered at the time. Suffice it to say, many factors hindered the full acceptance of the citrus remedy.[7]

Innovation often diffuses slowly. Many factors, often unexplainable, contribute to this resistance. Deal tenderly with church members as you present the cell-church vision. Give people sufficient time to process the new ideas, and carefully explain how the cell church will benefit their lives. Adopting new ideas takes time, and there is always potential for conflict. Learning how to manage change dynamics will help you work through the conflict and establish the cell-church philosophy as the new norm in your church.

15

Take Deliberate Steps to Become a Cell Church

When my wife and I arrived in Costa Rica in April 1990, we were as green as gringos could be. Instead of saying, *Quisiera cononcerte*, "I would like to get to know you," I would say, *Quisiera cocinarte*, "I would like to cook you." Some of my more hilarious Spanish blunders are not repeatable in public.

I began to learn Spanish when I was 33. Sorting out the foreign Spanish sounds was difficult for me. To compensate for my lack of natural talent, I had to study hour upon hour. Like a child, I learned the importance of following grammar rules, the logic of the Spanish language. Taking time in the beginning has had a lasting, long-term impact on my ministry in Ecuador.

You might be as green to cell-church philosophy as I was to the Spanish language. Study each of the following steps and implement them one at a time. If you're a seasoned pro, concentrate on those steps most applicable to your situation.

STEP ONE: MAKE SURE THE SENIOR PASTOR IS IN AGREEMENT

Don't even try the cell-church approach unless the senior pastor is totally involved. Many zealous laypeople long to introduce cell changes, but they won't work unless the senior pastor takes responsibility. An enthusiastic layperson might convince the pastor and the church to embark on cell ministry. The change might even take hold, but without the senior pastor guiding the transition, the church will be a church with cells. Cell churches require total participation by the senior pastor.

Through experience, I've learned the wisdom behind Cho's advice, "… ministers [senior pastors] must be personally committed to small groups. They must have personal knowledge, personal interest, and personal leadership in the small-group system."[1]

Shane Crawford once shared an excellent illustration describing the senior pastor's role in transitioning to the cell-church paradigm. He likened a cell-church transition to a train changing tracks. The lead train (head pastor) changes tracks first, and the supporting engines (key leaders) follow. For a while, the train is both on the old track (program church) and the new one (cell church). This is not a problem because the members are following the leadership. Crawford concludes, "The church's transition must begin with the lead engine (the senior pastor)."[2]

STEP TWO: ANALYZE YOUR CHURCH

Self-analysis is one of the major places where churches miss the boat. People need to understand the present health of their church before they consider changes. Leaders get so excited about the cell-church vision that they lose sight of the fact that the present state of their church hinders this type of transition. Is your church a praying church? Are members open to change or do they resist every innovation? Is your church outreach-oriented or inward-looking? Reflect on these questions as you consider transitioning into the cell model. Identifying the principal barriers will help ease your cell-church transition. The healthier the church, the easier the transition. But if the church hasn't changed in 200 years and only wants to be fed and "feel" the Spirit, then the leader must not expect immediate results.

A church cannot move from A to C without going through B. It also cannot move to C without knowing what A is. Understanding where you are at the present is a preliminary step for introducing change. Thinking about change starts with seeing the situation as it is now. Only afterward can you envision what you want to become.

Our cell-church transition was preceded by a 40-page analysis of the church. We analyzed our current growth patterns and ministries, noting both strengths and weaknesses. This study helped everyone see the cracking infrastructure. It compelled us to confront problems in key areas, although we had continually grown numerically on Sunday mornings. The analysis also prepared us for potential difficulties. It became apparent that as a church with cells, we were sliding into "Sunday club" status. The study revealed that we needed to change our staff structure, our equipping system, and other key areas. After seeing these facts, the key leaders climbed on board.

This type of analysis doesn't have to be complicated. I recommend four sections:

1. Background of your church, the history and context,
2. Growth patterns, including statistics for attendance, membership, finances, etc., for the last five to 10 years,
3. Evaluation of current ministries, noting both the positive and negative aspects,

4. Recommendations of future cell-church goals in light of #1 through #3 (see Step Four in this chapter for more detail).

There are a few principles to remember as you analyze your church. First, make prayer the priority. It must be the foundation for all that you do. Only He can point out exactly what is needed for a successful transition.

Second, your church doesn't have to change its unique identity to become a cell church. You are not Faith Community Baptist Church, Bethany World Prayer Center, or the International Charismatic Mission. You are who you are by God's sovereign plan. Don't throw away the years of positive qualities of your church. For example, are you missions-oriented? Refine this feature through your cell ministry. Do you have a strong Christian Education program? Use it to perfect your children's cells and celebration. Are you known for your social outreach? Improve this emphasis through your cell-church ministry.

Third, don't assume that everything must change right away. Only when a healthy cell system is in place will you want to begin major alterations of the traditional structure. Some of your current ministries can refocus to support the cell structure rather than compete with it. It's a mistake to assume that all programs are wrong. Even the early church had some "programmatic" elements, such as the food-distribution program mentioned in Acts 6 and the relief program recounted in Acts 11. Most churches will need to eliminate many programs, however, because they drain the energy, leadership, and prayer focus of the church.

STEP THREE: ANALYZE OTHER CELL CHURCHES

Take time to research before implementing changes. You need to know what you want the church to look like. This book and others will help you envision your future cell-church structure, but visit other cell churches if possible.

I counsel pastors to MAKE THE TIME to attend a cell conference at Bethany World Prayer Center. Why? Because you need to see a cell church. It's one thing to hear about cell churches; it's quite another to see and experience one.

Our senior pastor at the Republic Church, Porfirio Ludeña, graciously assented to our cell-church transition in the early stages. But he didn't take hold of the cell-church philosophy until he visited the International Charismatic Mission. He returned a change man. Then we couldn't hold him back. Next he visited the Elim Church in El Salvador. Seeing isn't always believing, but it sure helps.

Bethany World Prayer Center is the leading cell church in the U.S. Bethany is on the cutting edge primarily because of its willingness to learn from other fast-growing churches around the world. Bethany has sent its leaders to capture principles from cell churches in Colombia, El Salvador, Korea, and Singapore. Is it any wonder that more than 1,000 pastors attend Bethany's annual cell seminars?

One church in Alaska spent $30,000 to train its staff at the beginning of its cell-church transition. This church spared nothing to equip the staff with knowledge and skills necessary for a successful transition. You probably won't spend that much; maybe you'll spend more. The key is willingness. Are you willing to do what is necessary to make your cell transition work?

STEP FOUR: ENVISION WHAT YOU WANT TO BECOME

World-class athletes frequently envision the final act of their events before it actually happens. They go through the event twice: once in their mind as a way of "seeing" it perfectly, and secondly when it actually happens. They make decisions in the present based on that envisioned event. These athletes discipline themselves in the present as a result of projecting themselves mentally into the future.

Likewise, you need to envision the final state of your cell-church transition before you start. You need a clear picture of the mature state. To merely hope that the result will be positive is not enough; rather, a proven, "mature template" is needed so that it can be followed throughout the entire process.

Write down the situation as it is right now, and then write down the situation as you can see it in the future (as part of your church analysis, explained in Step Two). Leaders with vision from God should be able to see what the THEN situation will be like. Leaders who dream about the THEN are able to interpret present happenings in terms of this future state, which they envision as already having taken place. They can live in the tension of what shall be, as if it were happening in the present.

STEP FIVE: WIN SUPPORT THROUGH RELATIONSHIP-BUILDING

Experts on change dynamics advise that developing relationships is key to the entire change process. Good ideas alone rarely convince people of the need for change. Relationships with people are the key. If people who will ultimately accept, adapt, or reject proposed changes don't believe in you (the change agent), they are also likely to reject your proposed changes. You must, therefore, build relationships in order to establish credibility for the changes that you hope to make.

People are influenced by friends, not by experts. This also holds true for those who are highly educated. If you want to influence people and guide them to the desired change, become their friend. Spend time with them. Drink lots of coffee with people. Get ready, because it's going to take time.

Ask yourself these questions:

- Have I consistently communicated love and care to the church?
- Do the members feel genuinely loved by me?
- Do I have a surplus relational balance, or is my account overdrawn?[3]

Many pastors who have successfully transitioned churches began the process with a high surplus balance in their relational bank account. Leading people into change drains the surplus balance. If a pastor and leadership team are operating in a negative balance, they should make deposits into the account before transitioning.

Relationship-building is important at all levels and with all people. But during a time of transition, it's especially important that the movers and shakers of the church support the plan. While God created all men equally, some have more influence than others. Every church has its power people. These are the ones who move policy, often behind the scenes. Without their nod of approval, little happens. Leader, you might not like this, but you need to live with it. You must win these people to your cell-church philosophy to guarantee long-term success. You can win a few battles without them, but you won't win the war. As one leader described his relationship with the power people: "I am their leader so I follow them. As soon as I find out where they want to go, I'll stand at the head of the line so I don't look bad."[4]

Take your church board, for example. If they're not participating in cells, they will eventually sink the ship. Every key leader must embrace the vision in order to successfully transition. At the Republic Church, people cannot serve on the board unless they are leading a cell group.

But what if your movers and shakers haven't accepted the vision? First talk with them and lead them into a clear understanding of what the church will look like if it transitions into the cell model. Ralph Neighbour Jr. recommends taking these people on a retreat.[5] These power people might come from one of the five groups of change agents:

Innovators: true change agents
Early Adopters: very open to change
Early Majority: ahead of the rest but want to maintain steady
        transition
Later Majority: more traditional and less open to change
Laggards: resist change

If your power people are in the Innovator or Early Adopter categories, you can proceed with changes quite rapidly; if they are mainly in the Early Majority category, you must proceed with caution; if they are in the Late Majority or Laggard categories, it's best not to even transition into the cell-church model.[6]

STEP SIX: BEGIN WELL

Be leery of textbooks that tell you EXACTLY what kind of transition model you must use in the early stages of your cell-church transition. Your situation is highly unique. And it rarely works the way the text dictates. Think of yourself as writing your own textbook on starting a cell-church ministry in the future.

There is no simple model that all successful pastors use to transition. A lot depends on your situation. Are you planting a church or trying to transition a traditional church? Do you have authority as the pastor or do you have to submit everything to your board? Are you the founder of your church or the seventh man down the line? Here are the two general routes that churches have used in transition.

The "Go for It" Approach

I mention this transition "model" because I've observed churches that broke all the rules and did it this way. A word of caution: Only a few U.S. churches have successfully launched cell ministry in this way.

The churches who successfully implemented the "Go for It" approach were led by strong, visionary pastors. Their authority and vision in the church made their cell-church dream a reality. Bethany World Prayer Center, for example, started 54 cells at once, which in six months multiplied to 108.[7] Yes, Pastor Larry prepared these leaders beforehand, but he charted his own course. At the same time, few pastors have the authority of Larry Stockstill. His people submit to his lead.

Jerry Smith, senior pastor of the Christian Center in Guayaquil, Ecuador (2,000 cell groups), started 16 groups at once in 1991 and in less than one year grew to 90. By 1993 there were 288 cell groups. Pastor Smith is a risk-taker. He attempts great things for God and expects great things from God.

Pastor Sergio Solórzano, founder of the Elim Church in San Salvador, was even more radical. He returned from visiting Cho's church in 1985 and was so on-fire for cell ministry that he immediately closed all 25 daughter churches around San Salvador in order to create one large, mother cell church. By 1991, the cell-group attendance had grown to 57,000, with a large proportion attending the Sunday celebration services.

There are striking similarities in the above examples:

- The senior pastor was the founder and unchallenged leader and enjoyed a high surplus of goodwill from the people.[8]
- The senior pastor did his homework beforehand (normally by visiting a cell church) and understood cell-church ministry.

- The senior pastor prepared key leaders before starting the transition.
- The cell-church vision was effectively communicated to the rest of the church.
- The church was already comparably healthy before starting the transition.

The Model-Group Approach

This approach starts small and then builds exponentially. It begins with a prototype, which according to the dictionary is "an original type, form, or instance that serves as a model on which later stages are based or judged." The first model group is led by the senior pastor of the church. It usually includes staff members and key influencers in the church.

Recently a pastor approached me asking, "Will you come to our church and do a seminar on cell ministry? We're a 30-year-old church that has been in a continual state of decline. After reading your manual, I'm convinced that cells are the answer." I sensed the sincerity and even desperation in his voice, but I also knew that a cell seminar wouldn't solve the church's woes. So I said, "Gather the 10 willing leaders you've already recruited into a model small group. Lead this group for at least three months, so that everyone experiences cell values. In the meantime, preach cell values to the congregation. Prepare the church. After you've modeled cell life to those 10, and they launch their own cell groups, I'll be glad to teach a cell seminar in your church."

I invited this senior pastor to attend my cell group while he was leading those 10 future leaders. Why? So he could also experience cell life. Most leaders of traditional churches don't understand cell values. They've never led a cell group. To launch a cell ministry without experiencing the life of the cell would lead the church down the wrong path.

The Model-Group Approach says that small-group ministry is better caught than taught. Rather than starting the transition by teaching the people about cell ministry, this approach allows the leaders to experience cell ministry first. Those initial leaders then impart what they've experienced in a small group to others in the church. William Beckham says: "The senior leader must model the community he is expecting everyone else to live in. If leaders don't have the time to live together in cell life, how can they expect members to do it?[9]

Mistakes made in the prototype stage are more easily corrected before they spread throughout a group system. Key leaders are part of the process from the beginning, making it more likely that they will actively support small-group ministry. If the prototype group does not practice evangelism, neither will any of the resulting groups. If prototype group leaders do not model leadership development, neither will any of the other leaders.

Dale Galloway, for example, started his small-group church by forming and leading the initial group in his home. Out of that initial group, he trained leaders for the next groups who passed on the vision to new leadership.[10] Even Jesus started by forming His own prototype cell. He spent years developing the model. He couldn't afford failure.

Although Cho has a church of over 700,000 members, he counsels new cell-church pastors to start small: "Take a dozen key lay leaders and train them as cell leaders. Then have them form their own home cell meetings, and watch over them carefully for six to eight months. Once this group of cells has begun to bear fruit, it will be time to get the whole church involved."[11]

After a certain period, the prototype group releases the original members as leaders of their own groups. How long before this happens? I recommend between three and six months.[12] What's important is for you to have a date, a goal for your original leadership cell to multiply. Before entering the senior pastor's model cell, all potential leaders must commit to leading their own cell group in three to six months.

STEP SEVEN: END WELL

While the prototype is being developed, the pastor begins preaching and teaching on the values and the vision of cell ministry. He prepares the congregation for the process of change by proclaiming kingdom values for all Christians.

At some point, initiate a cell seminar so the rest of the church becomes involved with the cell-church strategy. This seminar will serve as a fishing pool for future cell leadership. Those in the seminar will attend the new groups started by the members of the prototype group.[13]

As you progress in your cell-church transition, follow the guidelines proposed in this book:

- Concentrate on your cell ministry in the face of competing programs (Chapter 8);
- Develop your system of oversight and support (Chapter 10);
- Establish an equipping system to train new leaders (Chapter 11);
- Fine-tune your cell church by paying attention to details (Chapter 12);
- Provide a first-class celebration service (Chapter 13).

CONCLUSION

Desire + preparation = successful transition. Meditate on the principles outlined in this chapter, analyze your unique church situation, and make use of your God-given creativity.

Skyscrapers capture our attention because of their immensity and beauty, but most of us think little about their foundation. But architects and construction workers give them much regard and time.

Christian leader, give careful prayer and thought to your cell-church foundation. Prepare the groundwork, do your homework, and you will succeed.

16

LEARN FROM

MARK MCGWIRE

It was a million-dollar baseball. Tim Forneris, a grounds crewmember working the left field stands, found it. Police were on hand to protect whoever caught it. Published reports said the ball could be worth as much as $2 million to collectors.

What was so special about this baseball? Mark McGwire hit it. With that hit, his 62nd homerun, McGwire toppled the 37-year-old homerun record held by Roger Maris. Babe Ruth had previously held the record for 34 years. "It was a sweet, sweet run around the bases," McGwire said after the game. "I will tell you the last week and a half my stomach has been turning, my heart has been beating a million miles a minute."

Mark McGwire, like the rest of us, started small. He didn't become a homerun king overnight. He started his training in Little Leagues, where he learned to swing a bat and run the bases. But as he persevered and followed time-tested principles, McGwire hit 70 homeruns in one season and thus broke baseball's most cherished record.

Most of you haven't arrived in the majors — yet. As you read about world-renown cell churches that are constantly breaking records, remember that all of these churches started in the minor leagues. They experimented, tested, and learned from others, and they continue to do so. Follow their principles, but you'll have to start from the beginning, in the minors.

People are excited about the cell model because it works, providing maximum church growth without sacrificing quality. Just as the early church, which emphasized cell and celebration, modern-day cell churches grow exponentially and endlessly.

To experience similar results, you must dig deep and build a strong foundation. Start now to lay the underpinnings that will serve your cell church in the future. Pay attention to details. Rely on the Spirit of God through prayer. Always remember that dynamic cells thrive in a nourishing environment. As you prepare your leaders well, give careful thought to your structure and concentrate on cell ministry, you'll begin to see similar fruit.

God desires your church to grow both in quality and quantity. It's not His will that anyone should perish, but He desires that all might come to repentance and receive the Good News of the Gospel. God will use your church to reap the harvest. Your church can grow because God desires it.

THE 5x5 MODEL:
THE ELIM CHURCH

After traveling to Korea to analyze David Yonggi Cho's church, Pastor Sergio Solórzano, founding pastor of the Elim Church, transformed his church into a cell church. Although EC generally follows the organizational system of David Cho's church in Korea, it also has adapted its system according to the Latin American context.

When the transition began in 1985, the mother EC church immediately closed 25 affiliated EC churches in order to create one cell church in San Salvador. Since that time, the organizational system has developed according to its needs.

CELL ADMINISTRATION

The system of cell administration at Elim is patterned after the Jethro model used in most cell churches around the world. It is geographically based on districts and zones. The cell groups must multiply within those geographical areas, and newcomers are assigned to groups according to where they live rather than their homogeneity.

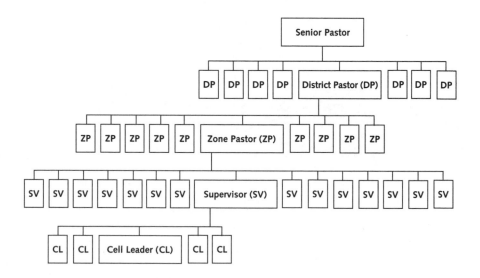

There are eight district pastors and 57 zone pastors at EC. Each district pastor has approximately 675 groups under his care (about 14,500 people). The zone pastor oversees the 15 to 20 supervisors under his care. It is not uncommon for a zone pastor to be responsible for 100 groups and between 1,000 and 1,500 people. It is truly a full-time job.

LEADERSHIP FUNCTIONS

Cell leadership at Elim believe that they must exemplify cell ministry. All top leadership is involved in the battle. No one dictates. No one is elevated in cell ministry at Elim unless he has succeeded at lower levels. All of them have moved up the ladder. All district pastors and zone pastors are paid staff members at Elim. There are 65 full-time pastors and one head pastor.

Head Pastor

The Elim manual makes it very clear that the pastor is the key success factor in the cell ministry. He must not delegate his pivotal role to anyone. He must never delegate so much that he ends up losing touch with the cell system.

The head pastor meets with the district pastors and zone leaders every Tuesday at 8 A.M. to encourage, pray and motivate. By late Monday or early Tuesday, the senior pastor receives statistics concerning cell growth during the previous week. Also he attends one of the cell groups every Saturday night in order to keep in touch with what is happening.

District Pastor

The district pastor is responsible for his entire district — approximately 675 cells groups and 14,500 people. The district pastor principally works with his 12 zone pastors to care for the district. He is regularly involved in preaching and administering the sacraments for his particular district.

I was also impressed that the district pastor must be in one cell planning meeting each week and one cell group each week. Normally he accompanies one of the zone pastors to the meeting. In this way, the district pastor never loses touch with the day-to-day reality of the cell philosophy.

Zone Pastor

The zone pastor oversees about 30 supervisors. Each supervisor has some five groups in his or her particular zone. He might have 15 to 30 supervisors under his care. For this reason it is not uncommon for a zone pastor to be responsible for 100 groups and between 1,000 and 1,500 people. The pastor visits his supervisors and cell leaders, preaches during the mid-week service, and administers the sacraments to his zone. Unlike in some cell churches, the zone pastors at Elim are not pressed to visit a set number of people. They do what it takes to assure that their zone grows.

Zone pastors must rotate among the groups each week. On Thursday night he visits a planning meeting in the district. On Saturday he is in a cell group. He maintains a constant watchfulness over the cell ministry.

Supervisor

The role of supervisor is not a paid position at Elim. Women can be supervisors but only over women groups. The supervisor has some five required meetings that he or she must attend each week. The chief role of the supervisor is to care for the five cell groups under his or her care. To assure quality control, the supervisor rotates among the groups on Thursday and Saturday nights.

Cell Leader

At Elim each leader has only one group. The goal of the cell leader is to multiply the group. In order to do this, the team approach is used. Everyone in the cell group has a particular role (leader, assistant, host, secretary, treasurer, children's leader, and members-at-large). Sometimes a supervisor oversees a group more directly until a new leader is found, but this is not too common.

UNIQUE CHARACTERISTICS OF THE CELL SYSTEM

EC has practically set the standard for the 5x5 model in Latin America.[1] The organization of every aspect of church life is accomplished through the cells. The only way for a person to be involved in any type of service ministry is to faithfully be involved in a cell group.[2] Some of the key organizational points are discussed below:

Penetration Strategy

One of the major purposes of the cell groups is to penetrate non-Christian territory and to prepare the ground for non-Christians to belong to the church. The goal is always to have a number of people in the "pipeline" who are potential church members.[3]

100 Percent Growth Goal

EC has maintained the goal of doubling the cell groups and cell membership each year. One of the reasons all cell groups have the same goal is so that the leadership is on the same statistical level. The other reason is to provide an ambitious goal that motivates the cell leadership.[4]

Competition Among Cell Leadership

All leaders (e.g., cell leaders, supervisors, zone leaders and district leaders) are ranked according to how close they come to annually doubling the number of cell groups, cell attendance, cell conversions and cell baptisms.[5] Each leader is placed on a list that compares his percentage growth to that of his co-leaders.[6] The purpose of these comparisons is to stimulate growth and create a "healthy competition."[7] The growth statistics are compiled on the following forms:

Cell Leader Form
- Cell leaders or cell secretaries must complete this form after each meeting on Saturday night and give it to the secretary by Sunday morning.
- The form consists of cell code, place, and hour of meeting, attendance in cell, attendance in church, conversions, reconciliations, baptism in water and Spirit, offering (church and bus), and place for two signatures (leader and host).

Supervisor Form

- On Sunday, the supervisors complete one general form that synthesizes the information from the cell forms and present it to the zone pastor.

Zone Pastor Form

- On Monday, the zone pastors synthesize the information from each supervisor's form and enter it into the computer (one computer in each district office).

District Pastor Form

- On Monday, the district pastor gives a synthesis of the results from his zone pastors. He hands those results to the administration.
- The administration hands a summary of all weekly statistics to the head pastor by Tuesday morning.

Orderly Statistical Administration

Latin Americans are often labeled as not being particularly organized or statistically oriented. This is certainly not true at EC. They have developed a highly efficient system of statistical tracking that is entirely indigenous.[8] The above forms illustrate the process of tracking statistical data.

Emphasis on Team Leadership

The church strongly emphasizes team leadership in the cell group, and this is a very positive point about the cell system at EC. Besides the leader, each group is encouraged to have an assistant, host, treasurer, secretary, instructor of children and members-at-large. The cell leader strives to form the core team to ensure a successful multiplication.

Planning Meetings on Different Night

Perhaps this aspect of having two separate cell meetings (one for planning and one for outreach) is the major distinction between the system at EC and other cell systems. EC requires that the cell teams meet on Thursday night for edification and planning. The purpose of the Thursday night planning meeting is to set the goals and receive the vision for Saturday night. One important function of the Thursday meeting is to encourage team members to visit those who were not present at the previous Saturday night cell group meeting. Core team members are assigned to visit these absent members.

Rotation Among Hosts

Although there is an official host of the group in whose house the group normally meets, people are encouraged to rotate the meeting place of the cell group. The specific goal of this strategy is to provide better opportunities for each member to invite relatives and non-Christians to their own home.[9]

Bus Ministry

EC is a citywide church. Their goal is to reach the two million inhabitants of San Salvador. Because most people do not have cars and the church is on the outskirts of the city, transportation is a major factor. EC deals with this problem by hiring over 600 buses to transport the 30,000 plus people to the celebration service and then back home again. The cell groups themselves take offerings to charter these city buses.

Study Guides

I was very impressed with the prepared cell lessons that EC produces. These guides provide three months of cell material. These lessons follow the expository preaching schedule of the midweek service at EC in order to provide continuity.[10]

Effective Children's Ministry

EC ministers to over 60,000 children every week in cell groups. The children's groups meet at the same time as the adult cells, in another room of the house. Normally, either one member of the planning team will sense a calling to teach the children or there might be a rotation among the planning team members. No set curriculum is used. Rather, the instructor is free to choose.

THE G-12 MODEL:
BETHANY WORLD PRAYER CENTER

For a long time, BWPF featured only family groups in a 5x5 geographical system. The family group emphasis helped them to start strong. Bethany still utilizes the geographical system and family cells are still the "bread-and-butter" small groups. Now, however, the Touch cells can launch homogeneous groups within the geographical boundaries.

Of the over 400 new groups that have recently started at Bethany World Prayer Center, approximately 90 percent are homogeneous groups. These groups are based on special interests such as sports, work or school. Bethany realizes that in American society today, most people find meaningful relationships at the workplace rather than in the neighborhood. People are most likely to get involved with those whom they know already. Thus, homogeneous groups are an effective way to evangelize and disciple non-Christians.

Basically, Bethany has broadened the scope of how groups can start. They still have the same basic goals of building relationships with God, with one another, and to reach the lost. They've taken away the ceiling. Now there are very few limits for starting new groups. The emphasis is on flexibility.

The new groups can fit into any time frame. If they have only 30 minutes for lunch, that's OK. They don't have to finish the whole lesson. Most leaders who start homogeneous groups form them at their workplace or school. A homogeneous leader has a dual commitment. He must lead his own cell group as well as receive discipleship in his original cell group during the week. To avoid schedule conflict, Bethany asks its leaders to limit the homogeneous groups to times when they are already meeting with people.

PRINCIPLES OF THE G-12 MODEL PRACTICED AT BWPC

Everyone is a potential leader

Bethany believes that every person has the potential to lead a cell group. Many first need to be healed (called soul therapy) and trained, but everyone is looked upon as a potential leader. Every person who walks in the church can be delivered from any type of bondage and prepared to lead a cell group.

Everyone Can Disciple 12 People

Bethany believes that the principle of 12 is a leadership training principle. When Bethany arrived at 300 cell groups, the church ran out of leaders. Since adopting the G-12 model, they've grown to 800 groups in approximately two years.

Each leader seeks out his 12 disciples. Brother Larry also has his disciples.[1] The district pastors, zone pastors and section leaders have a goal of leading 12 people to the Lord. They scan the congregation to discover potential disciples to add to their 12.

Bill Satterwhite, zone pastor of District One, converted his six section leaders into disciples. He started with those six. But he also looked around for other men to add to his group. He told me that he was specifically looking for people of the church who are not in groups but have leadership potential. One in his discipleship group was a past cell leader who had dropped out.[2] His goal is to gather 12 disciples into his group, train them, and eventually feed them into the system.

Billy Hornsby highlights that each member's lifetime goal of reaching as many people as possible requires him to do three things:[3]

1. Win 12 who become part of his group,
2. Disciple 12 in mentoring relationships,
3. Help each of his 12 to open a group and build their own groups of 12.

So the goal of every cell leader is to send each of his or her cell members to start their own cell groups. When that goal is reached, the original cell becomes a leadership meeting.[4]

Everyone Is Ministered To and Then Ministers

Everyone needs a group where they are ministered to, and then they need a group where they minister. Two times a week, each person forms part of a cell. Yes, this is a higher-level commitment. To compensate, they closed the Sunday night service, a break with a 32-year tradition! Now quite a few cells meet on Sunday night. They also made the Wednesday night expository meeting optional.

At Bethany, every cell leader is expected to attend at least two meetings a week. He leads his own cell group, but he also meets with his mother cell and receives discipleship from his original cell leader. The meeting with this person might occur 30 minutes before the normal cell begins or 30 minutes afterward. In that 30 minutes, mentoring occurs between cell leader and disciple. The top leadership at BWPC advise the leaders to make the meeting with the 12 as convenient as possible. Pastor Stockstill describes the circle of 12 as more of a "huddle for leaders" rather than some kind of heavy discipleship commitment.

An added benefit is that multiplication occurs without division. The new cell leader never really leaves his original group. He will also attend the cell meeting, thus taking away any sting of separation from the cell group.

A Person Is in Your 12 Only After Opening a Cell Group

Pastor Larry is emphatic that "no one should be in your 12 until they open a group."[5] He counsels senior pastors against appointing their board members as part of their 12. Fruitfulness in multiplication is a prerequisite. Billy Hornsby says, "When a new leader opens a group, he becomes part of the "permanent" 12 of his mentor. If I have 12 in my cell group, I'm just mentoring those people, but when the person opens a group, he becomes part of my permanent 12."[6]

Leadership training prepares a future leader to open his group and become part of your 12. Perhaps a cell group has 12 members. Your goal as a cell leader is to get each one of the members to enter the cell training process and to eventually become a cell leader.

Everyone Should Win Souls and Develop Potential Leaders

In the traditional Cho system, the zone pastor often becomes frustrated. He has to wait on cells to multiply. He has cells under him waiting for them to grow in attendance. Because attendance fluctuates, cell multiplication often never happens.

Under the G-12 system, you're not waiting for anybody. You're not trying to get attendance in cells but rather to raise-up leaders. You're not waiting on cells to multiply. Rather, you're pro-actively planting new cells through developed leadership. You're like a franchise distributor. They don't wait on one McDonald's to get so big that no one can go through the driveway. No, they decide where they want to open a McDonald's and simply do it. Likewise, in the G-12 approach, a new cell opens when a leader is ready to lead it.

When a person has found his or her 12, the goal becomes leadership development. If someone gets saved, that person is passed on to one of the groups of 12.

Your 12 Become Your Assistants in the Work

Those who form your 12 also become your assistants in cell ministry. One of the chief reasons for leadership burnout is not delegating responsibility. Often a leader feels that everything rests on his or her shoulders. One of the benefits behind developing 12 leaders is that they can share the ministry load.

APPENDIX C

CREATIVE COMBINATION MODEL:

FAITH COMMUNITY BAPTIST CHURCH

The organization of FCBC is important because it has a distinct niche in the cell church world. It combines the years of experience of cell expert Ralph Neighbour Jr. with the strong leadership of Lawrence Khong. This cell model is a pacesetter in the world today. FCBC is probably the most organized cell church that I have ever witnessed. Elim Church holds a close second. They are also the most reflective and articulate about their organization.

ADMINISTRATIVE STRUCTURE

For the most part, the leadership tree looks very similar to most cell churches. The senior pastor is at the top of the leadership tree. The district pastor is the next highest level in the cell system (although there is a "senior pastor's office," which consists of a few associate pastors). Under the district pastor is zone pastor. Both the district pastor and zone pastor are paid full-time by the church. The next level is the zone supervisor, who shepherds five cell groups (actually they have reduced this load to about three).

Division of Cell System

For me, it was worth the trip to Singapore just to discover such a creative, fresh organizational system. FCBC has combined the efficiency of the geographical district with the need for specialized ministry better than any other cell church.

Geographical Districts

These districts are described as homogeneous with heterogeneous cell groups. This simply means that the districts reach out to families who are culturally similar. These family groups are called "intergenerational cells" because they include children. District divisions encourage cells to reach out to near neighbors as well as to assimilate church converts who live nearby.

Campus and Combat District

This district serves college/university-age youth 18 to 25. Younger people from the youth zone graduate into this district after high school, and young adults older than 25 graduate into the district cells. Chua Seng Lee, Campus Combat Director, told me that only future workers are allowed to stay within his district after age 25. Pastor Lee establishes cells on university campuses as well as in military camps in Singapore. In this district, the standard FCBC cell lessons are adapted, leadership commitment is often shorter, and more cells are planted. Every six weeks, Pastor Lee gathers all of the cell members for a congregational service (about 600 attend).

Youth Zone

This zone reaches those ages 12 to 19. The Youth Zone requires more supervision. Instead of the normal ratio of one zone supervisor to five cells, the youth require one zone supervisor for every three youth cells. Instead of hosting evangelistic events, the youth cells evangelize through personal, relational evangelism.

Music Zone

Perhaps this zone is the most creative. It is comprised mainly of members from Touch Music Ministry. However, the cells are fully integrated with people not involved in the music ministry. Cell members are often friends of those in music ministry. Because of the demands of music ministry, leadership felt that integration between cell and ministry would be beneficial. I was impressed by the creativity of this arrangement. The reason why they are organized into a separate zone is so that those in the music ministry do not need to develop two sets of relationships. Since the music ministry involves considerable time commitment, this relieves some of the scheduling pressure and enables them to concentrate.

Chinese District

Although English unifies the four major languages spoken in Singapore, not everyone can speak English well. This district reaches out to non-English speakers through cells. It's also interesting that one entire worship service is dedicated to this language group every Sunday morning.

Handicap District

This district reaches out to the hearing-impaired, wheelchair-bound, intellectually disabled, and visually handicapped. This district office is organized with the same charts and procedures as the other districts.

I'm convinced that specialty districts are needed. Oftentimes, these special people do not feel wanted or cared for in normal geographical cell groups.

ADMINISTRATIVE SUPPORT

FCBC is one organized church! They are very professional about what they do. In the organizational chart, there exists one entire area called "administration support." This includes: Facilities (office planning, physical security, maintenance), Finance Department (accounting, budget planning, financial management), Human Resources (recruitment, benefits, employee relations, training of staff), and Ministry Information System (establishes the information technology within the church).

Like any well-organized, effective church, many specific needs must be met that cannot easily fit under the category of "cell." Some people like to label these activities as "evil programs." And sometimes these categories do become an end in themselves. However, even in the cell church, specialized ministries are essential. FCBC lists 10 specialized ministries.[1]

FCBC STAFF

The staff at FCBC is very large, efficient and well-organized. There are several characteristics worth noting.

Large Number
In April 1997, FCBC had far exceeded one goal: There was a paid staff member for every 2.5 cell groups (or one pastoral staff for every 4.5 cell groups). For every 30 people who attend FCBC, there is a staff member (or one pastoral staff for every 50 persons).[2]

This church has the highest staff-to-member proportion that I know.

Schedule
The entire staff prays each morning from 9 A.M. to 10 A.M. Staff planning and report collecting takes place on Tuesday. On this day, the staff spends two to three hours praying and worshipping together. On Wednesday, the senior pastor meets with the entire staff. Also on Wednesday, the district pastors meet with their staff. Once each month there is a half-day of prayer.

The last Saturday of each month at 2:30 P.M. all cell leadership meet together. Pastor Khong first meets with district pastors, zone pastors, zone supervisors and cell-group leaders. Afterwards, the leadership meets in districts. Zone pastors and zone supervisors meet together every two weeks. Pastor Khong encourages the staff "to play together." Retreats, recreation and time with family are high priorities.

Personal Cell Involvement
The senior pastor, associate pastor, and most district pastors and zone pastors participate in regular cell groups.[3] One district pastor also told me that he personally reads every cell report.

Cell Offices at FCBC
The cell offices are spread out over four locations. The core offices consist of three floors of an office building. Most of the district offices, the senior pastor's office and Touch Community Service are positioned in that complex. In another office complex about five minutes away, Touch Publications, the music district, youth district and TESS have their offices. At the church site, there are also a few administrative offices.

Statistical Control

FCBC is very statistically oriented. In the weekly Sunday bulletin, attendance for each service is recorded, as well as a cumulative and weekly financial report. FCBC requires a weekly report from every cell leader that may be faxed into the office. The zone supervisors diligently read the reports and pass them on to the district superintendent. One district pastor told me that he even reads the reports of every zone! I was told that more than just the statistics, the cell report provides information about the progress of the group.

Well-designed organizational charts hang on every district wall (often in several places). The monthly statistical progress of every cell, complete with the cell leader's photo, is part of each organizational chart.

NOTES

INTRODUCTION

[1] "Tent Of Meeting In Print" (May-August 1997). This article was published in *Joy* magazine (July 1997), 4. *Joy* is the official magazine of Assemblies of God in Great Britain and Ireland and is submitted with permission for Internet publication obtained from Peter Wreford, the editor (editor.newlife@hertz.ukonline.co.uk) July 31, 1997. Editorial office: New Life Publishing Co., PO Box 64, Rotherham, South Yorkshire S60 2YT.

[2] Ralph Winter quoted in Rick Wood's "Christianity Waning or Growing," *Mission Frontiers Bulletin*, (January-February 1993), 25.

[3] *Los Angeles Times*, 2 March 1996, Sec. B, pp. 4-5, quoted in Alan McMahan, "Church Resource Ministry's Refocusing Networks as a Systemic Church Growth Intervention," (Ph.D. tutorial, Fuller Theological Seminary, 1996), 37-38.

[4] McMahan, 4.

[5] Ralph W. Neighbour Jr., *Introductory Cell Church Seminar* presented in Miami, FL,1996 (TOUCH Outreach Ministries, Houston, TX), "Why the Holy Spirit Has Launched the Cell Church Movement," 2-3.

[6] Schwarz, Christian A., *Natural Church Development* (Carol Stream, IL: ChurchSmart Resources,1996), 32.

[7] The figures 35,000+ worshippers and 20,000 cell groups apply only to the mother church. There are an additional 10,000 worshippers and 7,000 cell groups in the 12 satellite churches around Bogota, thus totaling 45,000 worshippers and 27,000 cell groups.

[8] About 155,000 attend the mother church on Sunday. An additional 100,000 people attend the 14 YFGC satellite churches in different parts of Seoul, Korea. The 155,000 figure is

included in the chart because the 25,000 cell groups operate only in the mother church. It's unknown how many cells function in the 14 extension churches (official statistics at YFGC mention only the 25,000 cell groups of the mother church).

CHAPTER 1

[1] Richard Halverson, audiotape of message, World Relief, 1987.

[2] Ibid.

[3] Donald McGavran, *Understanding Church Growth*, 3rd ed. (Grand Rapids, MI: William Eerdmans Publishing Company, 1990), 22.

[4] The "back door" of a church refers to those who "exit" the church very soon after "entering." There are numerous reasons why people leave: lack of warmth, poor worship, inadequate nursery facilities, etc. "Closing the back door" refers to the church's ability to keep those who enter, thus experiencing church growth.

[5] C. Kirk Hadaway, Francis M. DuBose, and Stuart A. Wright, *Home Cell Groups and House Churches* (Nashville, TN: Broadman Press, 1987), 211.

[6] C. Peter Wagner, *Leading Your Church to Growth* (Ventura, CA: Regal Books, 1984), 20-21.

[7] McGavran, 254.

[8] Thomas Rainer, *The Book of Church Growth* (Nashville, TN: Broadman Press, 1993), 254.

[9] Ibid., 260-261.

[10] Schwarz, 32.

CHAPTER 2

[1] David Yonggi Cho, *Church Growth and the Home Cell System*, P.L. Kannaday, ed: (Seoul, Korea: Church Growth International, 1995), 22.

[2] Before visiting YFGC, I traced the influence of YFGC in seven other cell churches throughout the world. All of them were directly impacted by Pastor David Cho.

[3] Yoido Full Gospel Church, brochure, *The 16th Annual Church Growth International Conference*, (Seoul, Korea: Church Growth International, 1997), 2.

[4] YFGC does not use the terms "zone pastor" and "district pastor." They simply call them subdistrict leaders. I was also told that YFGC tries to minimize the distinction between district pastor and subdistrict pastors.

[5] Larry Stockstill, *The Cell Church* (Ventura: Regal Books, 1998), 51.

[6] Ibid., 22.

[7] The present facility is located less than one kilometer from the original 1977 meeting place, which is about 10 miles from downtown San Salvador.

[8] La Cosecha in Honduras (10,000 members), Christian Center in Guayquil (5,000 members), and Fe Esperanza y Amor in Mexico (10,000 members) have all structured their system after Elim Church. Bethany World Prayer Center in Lousiana also sends its pastors and workers to Elim to learn about cell ministry.

[9] This church has stretched my understanding of the organizational capabilities of Latin Americans. The organizational genius of EC is not a result of North American influence. I did not detect any such influence on Pastor Sergio or on the church in general. Rather, the church has reconditioned the Latin people to see the benefit of such tight informational control.

[10] Stockstill, 27.

CHAPTER 3

[1] Paul Yonggi Cho, *Successful Home Cell Groups* (Plainfield, NJ: Logos International, 1981), 107.

[2] Schwarz, 68.

[3] Billy Hornsby, *Implementing LDT*, audiotape, Bethany World Prayer Center, 1996.

[4] In the majority of these cell churches, celebration attendance is seen as a natural by-product of cell life. All cell members are expected to attend the celebration service; yet the leadership doesn't proclaim the church's attendance goals before the congregation. Christian Schwartz shares a similar discovery in *Natural Church Development*. I believe strongly in quantitative attendance goals, but I'm no longer certain whether the public proclamation of Sunday attendance goals helps the congregation to grow because it's difficult to designate responsibility for achieving such goals. Who is responsible if it does or doesn't happen? The congregation, the pastor, the board, everyone? However, goals for cell multiplication are first made by the leadership team (district pastors, zone pastors, etc.), and then proclaimed to the congregation to stir vision and excitement. New cell-group goals can then be carefully monitored throughout the year.

[5] César Castellanos, *Sueña y Ganarás el Mundo* (Bogotá, Colombia: Vilit Editorial, 1998), 172-174.

[6] Love Alive in Tegucigalpa, Honduras, reports this percentage.

[7] Cho, *Successful Home Cell Groups*, 93.

[8] Ibid., 107.

[9] Ralph W. Neighbour Neighbour Jr., *Where Do We Go From Here* (Houston, TX: Touch Publications, Inc., 1990), 73-80 (1990: 73-80).

[10] I am referring here to pastors, district leaders, zone leaders, supervisors, cell leaders, and administration.

[11] ICM, EC and CCG even use the home to hold cell groups for children, and all of the churches hold youth and adolescent ministries within the home.

[12] Stockstill, 29.

[13] The Elim Church follows the weekly midweek expository teaching and Yoido Full Gospel Church has created books of cell lessons that follow Cho's past sermons and expository teachings.

CHAPTER 4

[1] Michael Mack, *The Synergy Church* (Grand Rapids, MI: Baker Books, 1996), 55.

[2] César Castellanos, *Anointing for Multiplication*, audiotape of message given at Bethany World Prayer Center, November 1997.

[3] Claudia Castellanos, videotape of Friday morning cell seminar in Quito, Ecuador, May 1998.

[4] César Castellanos, "Exploring the Groups of Twelve," *Cell Church* VOL 7, no. 2 (Spring 1998), 24.

CHAPTER 5

[1] Larry Stockstill, *Partnership: A Relational Church*, audiotape, Bethany World Prayer Center, November 1997.

[2] Larry Stockstill, *Why Cells?: A Paradigm Shift*, audiotape, Bethany World Prayer Center, November 1997.

[3] Carl George, *Prepare Your Church for the Future* (Grand Rapids, MI: Fleming H. Revell, 1992), 13-14.

[4] Carl George, *How to Break Growth Barriers* (Grand Rapids, MI: Baker Book House, 1993), 88-97.

[5] George, *Prepare Your Church*, 67.

[6] Stockstill, *The Cell Church*, 44.

[7] Ibid., 26.

[8] *The New International Dictionary of the New Testament*, Colin Brown, ed., Vol. II (Grand Rapids: Zondervan, 1975), s.v. "house."

[9] Glen Martin and Gary ICMntosh, *Creating Community* (Nashville, TN: Broadman & Holman Publishers, 1997), 140.

[10] George, *How to Break*, 136.

[11] George Hunter III, *Church for the Unchurched* (Nashville, TN: Abingdon Press, 1996), 48.

[12] Everett M. Rogers, *Diffusion of Innovations*, 4th ed. (New York: The Free Press, 1995), 406.

CHAPTER 6

[1] When the missionaries left the country in 1949, there were one million Christians. Today conservative estimates places the number of believers at over 50 million and as high as 100 million people.

[2] F.F. Bruce, *The Epistles to the Ephesians and Colossians* in *The New International Commentary on the New Testament* (Grand Rapids, MI: William B. Eerdmans Publishing Co., 1957), 310.

[3] Robert Banks, *Paul's Idea of Community* (Peabody, MA: Hendrickson Publishers, 1994), 42-43.

[4] John Mallison, *Growing Christians in Small Groups* (London: Scripture Union, 1989), 5.

[5] C. Kirk Hadaway, Francis M. DuBose, and Stuart A. Wright, Home Cell Groups and House Churches (Nashville, TN: Broadman Press, 1987), p. 40.

[6] Kenneth Latourette, *Beginnings to 1500*, Vol. 1 (New York: Harper & Row, 1975), 131.

[7] William Brown, "Growing the Church Through Small Groups in the Australian Context," (D.Min. dissertation, Fuller Theological Seminary, 1992), 37.

[8] Jim & Carol Plueddemann, *Pilgrims in Progress* (Wheaton, IL: Harold Shaw Publishers, 1990), 4.

[9] Martin Luther, "Preface to the German Mass and Order of Service," in *Luther Works*, Vol. 53, ed. Helmut T. Lehman, (Philadelphia, PA: Fortress Press, 1965), 63-64.

[10] Charles E. White, ed. "Concerning Earnest Christians: A Newly Discovered Letter of Martin Luther," *Currents in Theology and Mission*, 10 (5), 1983, 273-282.

[11] Ibid., 275.

[12] Quoted on the Small Group Network, http://www.smallgroups.com/quotes.htm. Accessed Saturday, May 23, 1998.

[13] Rick Warren, *The Purpose Driven Church* (Grand Rapids, MI: Zondervan Publishing House, 1995), 325-326.

CHAPTER 7

[1] Robert Wuthnow, *I Come Away Stronger: How Small Groups Are Shaping American Religion*

(Grand Rapids, MI: William B. Eerdmans Publishing Company, 1994), 370.

[2] Ibid., p. 371.

[3] In George's *Prepare Your Church For The Future*, Cho or Cho's church appears on 13 pages. In George's most recent book, *The Coming Church Revolution*, Cho is mentioned on nine pages. A similar pattern appears in Neighbour's book *Where Do We Go From Here?* and Galloway's book *20/20 Vision.*

[4] *Where Do We Go From Here?*, 68-69.

[5] Elizabeth Farrell, "Aggressive Evangelism in an Asian Metropolis," *Charisma* January 1996, 54-56.

[6] George, *Prepare Your Church For The Future*, 57-84.

[7] Chapter 6, entitled "Identify Your Mice," promotes the identification of any type of small group in the church. This is unique from most cell-based churches. However, very little is mentioned about this philosophy in *Prepare Your Church for the Future*.

[8] Carl George, *The Coming Church Revolution* (Grand Rapids, MI: Fleming H. Revell, 1994), 279-280.

[9] Ibid., 69-70.

[10] Ibid., 284.

[11] David Limiero, "Meta, Model, or Martyr? Three Approaches to Introducing a Small Groups Ministry in Your Church," July 1996. http://smallgroups.com/models07.htm. Accessed: May 22, 1998.

[12] I studied Willow Creek Community Church, Cincinnati Vineyard, Fairhaven Alliance Church, New Hope Community Church, Saddleback Community Church, and New Life Community Church. SCC doesn't use the term Meta Model, but its small-group system is similar to that of the other four. WCCC, CV and FAC all acknowledge that they are following the Meta Model. NHCC often uses the term "meta" in describing its ministry.

[13] Cincinnati Vineyard lists every small group on its bulletin boards.

[14] WCCC's Membership Service Manager, Wayne, shared this information (847-765-0070 ext. 358). His job is to provide information about Willow Creek to those interested.

[15] Linda has been working at Saddleback in small-group ministries for the past four years.

[16] Lyman Coleman, *Serendipity Leadership Conference Syllabus* (Littleton, CO: Serendipity Publishers, 1993), Sec. 4, 17.

[17] Ibid.

[18] Ibid., Sec. 2, p. 21.

[19] ibid., Sec. 4, p. 21.

[20] Ted Haggard at New Life Church in Colorado Springs, CO. He calls his cell groups Free Market Cells. These cells (or Meta-type small groups) last one semester and then the members are given a choice to continue or to find another cell. Haggard touts the superiority of this model because of its "easy entrance and easy exit" policy (Ted Haggard, *The Life Giving Church* Ventura CA: Regal Books, 1998, 18). Haggard does say that the goal is long-term relationships.

[21] Coleman, Sec. 4, p. 13.

[22] Hestenes is well-known for her expertise in small-group ministry and in particular for being the spokeswoman for the Covenant Model. She received her doctorate from Fuller Theological Seminary and served as a professor.

[23] Coleman, Sec. 4, p. 5.

[24] Ibid.

[25] Ibid., p. 7.

[26] Ibid.

[27] BWPC web site-www.bccn.com, Wednesday, May 20, 1998.

[28] In the Cell Model, all these are necessary to comprise a cell. For instance, Pastor Larry Stockstill of Bethany World Prayer Center stopped calling his worship team meeting a cell group because they were not evangelizing non-Christians.

CHAPTER 8

[1] George Barna, *User Friendly Churches* (Ventura, CA: Regal Books, 1991), 51.

[2] Billy Hornsby, *Holding the Harvest* audiotape series (January 1998).

[3] Ibid.

CHAPTER 9

[1] Cho, *Successful Home Cell Groups*, 107.

[2] César Castellanos, *10 Commandments for Cell Groups*, videotape International Charismatic Mission (Bogota, Colombia, 1997).

[3] David Yonggi Cho made these comments during 1984 Church Growth lectures at Fuller Theological Seminary.

[4] Ralph Neighbour Jr., "The Cell Church Is a Praying Church," *Cell Church*, Vol. 3. No. 4 (Fall 1994), 19.

[5] Dale Galloway, *The Small Group Book* (Grand Rapids, MI: Fleming H. Revell, 1995), 21.

[6] David Yonggi Cho, *Church Growth Manual*, No. 7 (Seoul, Korea: Church Growth International, 1995), 23.

[7] Ibid., 27.

[8] Cho, *Church Growth and the Home Cell System*, 125.

[9] Cho, *Church Growth Manual*, No. 7, 21.

[10] Larry Kreider referred to this conversation with Cho during a panel discussion at the Post Denominational Seminar, Los Angeles, CA, May 22, 1996.

[11] Cho, *Successful Home Cell Groups*, 107.

CHAPTER 10

[1] For more detail, see the appendix, in which I've listed one model church for each major model (5x5, G-12, creative combination). My Ph.D. dissertation, "Cell-Based Ministry: A Positive Factor for Church Growth in Latin America," is available through TOUCH Publications, Houston, TX.

[2] Stockstill, *The Cell Church*, 47.

[3] Bethany World Prayer Center bases its geographical districts on ZIP codes.

[4] A remnant of the former geographical system remains (since ICM originally based its system on geography), but it is no longer promoted.

[5] Understand that this is the ideal but that the 5x5 numbering is not always observed. Elim, for example, had some eight-zone pastors (instead of five zones) under each district pastor.

[6] Ralph W. Neighbour Jr. "Structuring Your Church for Growth," *CellChurch*, Vol. 7, no. 2, 15.

[7] Ibid.

[8] The official name for the cells at ICM is "C.A.F.E." (Family Cells for Training and Evangelism).

[9] Pastor Alfonzo Ortiz, ex-secretary to César Castellanos, says that this can become a problem since a member of one group might feel attracted to another but might find it difficult to change groups.

CHAPTER 11

[1] George, *Prepare*, 98.

[2] Quoted in Ralph W. Neighbour Jr., "Barriers to Growth," *CellChurch* Vol. 6, no.3 (Summer 1997), 16.

[3] Ralph W. Neighbour Jr., *The Arrival Kit* (Houston, TX: Touch Publications, 1993) 11.

[4] Stockstill, *The Cell Church*, 86.

[5] George, *The Coming Church Revolution*, 84.

CHAPTER 12

[1] Stockstill, *The Cell Church*, 19.

[2] Advanced Cell Training Four Seminar (Houston, TX: TOUCH Outreach Ministries, Inc., 1998), p. 2 of Day 3, Session 3.

[3] George Barna, *The Power of Vision* (Ventura, CA: Regal Books, 1992), 143.

[4] In fact, we are changing the name of our "zones" to "networks." This reflects the affiliations or networks of groups that a specific pastor oversees.

[5] Bethany World Prayer Center and Faith Community Baptist Church did not take offerings.

[6] Larry Stockstill, *The Cell Church* (Ventura: Regal Books, 1998), p. 118.

[7] Larry Stockstill, *Questions and Answers*, audiotape, (Bethany World Prayer Center November 1997).

CHAPTER 13

[1] Schwarz, 31.

[2] Sunday services declare to cell members that even cell leaders receive pastoring. Members know that professional help is available for certain counseling situations, weddings, funerals, etc. Plus, in the celebration service, cell members are part of something greater than their individual cell. Cell churches depend on the higher-level pastoral staff to provide studies, train leaders, preach the Bible, and perform marriages and other pastoral functions.

[3] Most cell churches reserve the Lord's Supper and baptism for the celebration service, and this ministry load is shared among pastoral staff. Seven of the eight cell churches studied administer the sacraments during the celebration service, FCBC being the only exception. At FCBC the Lord's Supper takes place in individual cells. One major reason that most cell churches prefer the celebration atmosphere is because it helps avoid the "house church" distinction. Many cell churches are also hesitant to place cell leaders in the position of administrating the Lord's Supper in the cell because many cell leaders lack formal training and maturity. We must remember that cell leaders are facilitators, not formal pastors.

[4] A team from our church in Quito, Ecuador, recently visited Elim Church and reported that about 50 people receive Jesus Christ as Savior in each of the six Sunday worship services.

CHAPTER 14

[1] Lyle Schaller, *Parish Planning* as quoted in C.Kirk Hadaway, *Church Growth Principles: Separating Fact from Fiction* (Nashville, TN: Broadman Press, 1991), 111.

[2] Robert J. Clinton, *Bridging Strategies* (Altadena, CA: Barnabas Publishers, 1992), 2-13.

[3] Ibid.

[4] *Advanced Cell Training* seminar, (Houston, TX: TOUCH Outreach Ministries Inc., 1998), p. 2 of Day 3, Session 2.

[5] Ibid., p. 4 of Day 3, Session 1.

[6] Clinton, 2-10.

[7] Everett M. Rogers, *Diffusion of Innovations*, 4th ed. (New York: The Free Press, 1995), 7-8.

CHAPTER 15

[1] Michael Mack, "Six Reasons American Small-Group Ministries Fail," *Ministries Today* (May/June 1993).

[2] Shane Crawford, "Finally! A Simple Explanation," *Cell Church*, Vol. 7 no. 1 (Winter 1998), 12.

[3] *Advanced Cell Training*, 3 of Day 3, Session 2.

[4] Carl George, *How to Break Growth Barriers* (Grand Rapids: Baker Book House, 1993), 114.

[5] Ralph W. Neighbour, Jr. *Introductory Cell Church Seminary*, Miami: FL, 1996 (Houston, TX: Touch Outreach Ministries), pp. 2-6 of section entitled "Transitioning a Traditional Church to a Cell-Based Church."

[6] Ibid.

[7] Stockstill, *The Cell Church*, 21-22.

[8] I recognize that Larry Stockstill is the son of the founder (Roy Stockstill). Yet, the principle is the same. Pastor Roy passed down his authority to his son Larry and the congregation respected that transfer of authority.

[9] William A. Beckham, *The Second Reformation* (Houston, TX: Touch Publications, 1995), 168. On a side note, I recommend that all pastoral staff continue to lead their own cell group — even after becoming a full-fledged cell church. You need to continue to experience cell life and model it to your flock. If you can't multiply your cell, for example, how will you expect this of others.

[10] Galloway, 42.

[11] Paul Yonggi Cho, *Successful Home Cell Groups*, 111.

[12] According to Ralph Neighbour, Jr., after two months of training within the cell group, the original disciples will open their own cell groups.

[13] Ralph W. Neighbour, Jr. , "Transitioning a Traditional Church to a Cell-Based Church."

APPENDIX A: THE 5x5 MODEL: THE ELIM CHURCH

[1] I have noticed many aspects that other cell churches have copied from MCE.

[2] For example, all ushers are first recommended through the cell groups at MCE.

[3] For this reason, there are over 60,000 adults and 56,000 children in the cell groups as compared to 30,000 adults and 3,000 children in the church on Sunday morning.

[4] Although in the past few years, this goal has not even come close to being fulfilled, I was told that Latin leadership will normally only reach for what is expected. To lower the goal to fifty percent would cause them to reach for less.

[5] A certain weight is given to each category: new cell group growth is given thirty percent; cell

adult attendance growth--twenty-five percent; cell children attendance growth--five percent; cell conversion growth--twenty percent; cell baptismal growth--twenty percent. It should be noted that there are not percentage points given for success in bringing the group to church. In my opinion, this lowers the priority of promoting celebration attendance in the cell group.

[6] District pastors are compared to district pastors; zone pastors are compared within each district and also among all fifty-seven. Supervisors are compared within their zone. It must be remembered that all of these lists are updated on a weekly basis!

[7] No one wants to be at the bottom of the list. I was told that in this way, everything is out in the open and no one can hide.

[8] This reveals to me that Latin Americans can indeed work effectively in a highly organized statistical environment, without being overly pressured.

[9] The host must belong to the church and be converted. It is also required that the meeting take place in the same area, zone, and district in which the group is located. If a member who lives in another district wants to have the meeting in his home, that meeting would come under the jurisdiction of another district, and therefore this type of changing is not recommended.

[10] The guides reminded me of a devotional guide such as Daily Bread. Each lesson covers three pages. There is a Scriptural passage, a central theme, an introduction, body of message, and application. On Tuesday night the zone pastor meets with the supervisors, cell leaders, and cell assistants to teach them how to communicate the following lessons. In my opinion, the greatest weakness of these study guides is that there are no questions provided. In other words, it is a non-participative Bible study.

APPENDIX B: THE G-12 MODEL: BETHANY WORLD PRAYER CENTER

[1] I was told that Pastor Larry is currently working with the governor and his staff and is seeking to form them into his 12 disciples.

[2] Another of Bill Satterwhite's disciples moved to another part of the city and his cell dissolved. When he moved back to Baker, Bill invited to become part of his 12.

[3] Billy Hornsby, Audiotape called, "Activity: Maintenance-Growth." Holding the Harvest Series. January 1998.

[4] Larry Stockstill, *The Cell Church* (Ventura, CA: Regal Books, 1998), p. 100.

[5] Larry Stockstill, Tape called "Questions and Answers" from Bethany Cell Conference held in November 1997.

[6] Billy Hornsby, Audiotape called, "Activity: Maintenance-Growth." Holding the Harvest Series. January 1998.

APPENDIX C: CREATIVE COMBINATION MODEL: FAITH COMMUNITY BAPTIST CHURCH

[1] They include: Children's Ministry (support for intergenerational cells, training and resource center, in charge of the Sunday celebration for children), Counseling Ministry (equips members, leaders, and pastors with people-helping skills), Family Life Ministry (prepares young people for marriage, assists districts in the area of counseling), Mission Department (serves as mission resource center and assists the districts to fulfill the great commission), Prayer Ministry (establishes prayer shield for senior pastor's office, coordinates spiritual

warfare network in Singapore), Touch Community Services (an independent, non-profit organization to meet a variety of physical needs), Touch Equipping Stations System (helps cell districts and developing cell churches worldwide equip leadership), Touch Ministries International (encourages international network of cell churches), Touch Music Ministry (provides support for celebration services as well as to outreach efforts), and Touch Resource (provides cell equipping material).

[2] There are actually 118 pastoral staff and 77 administrative staff. Church growth theorists believe that a healthy staff balance is one per every 150 people.

[3] The cell can be located in any area. The zone pastors are less likely to participate in one cell since they rotate from cell to cell.

ADDITIONAL RESOURCES FROM TOUCH ON CELLS

HOME CELL GROUP EXPLOSION
by Joel Comiskey
Joel Comiskey traveled to eight of the most successful cell churches in eight countries to tell you how cells have reached millions for Christ. You will learn the keys for successful cell leadership and discover why cell groups multiply. Pastors can learn which elements predict growth in cells. Cell leaders will learn from the best cell leaders in the world and potentially join their ranks. Take your church and cell groups to a new stage of excitement. 152 pgs.

SHARPEN YOUR STRATEGY FOR A GREATER HARVEST
by Joel Comiskey
This one-hour video covers 10 principles necessary to achieve your cell-church vision. These truths can transform your leadership!

THE SECOND REFORMATION
by William A. Beckham
Don't jump head-first into a cell church transition or church plant without reading this book! Beckham brilliantly walks you through the logic of a cell/celebration structure from a biblical and historical perspective. He provides you with a step-by-step strategy for launching your first cells. This wonderful companion to Ralph Neighbour's material will ground you in the values and vision necessary for a successful transition to cells. 253 pgs.

SHEPHERD'S GUIDEBOOK
by Ralph W. Neighbour, Jr.
This thoroughly tested book will equip your cell leaders for success and train them to listen to God for their cell members, develop community and lead people into relationship evangelism. Not only will your cell leaders gain the tools for leading a cell meeting, they will also learn to pastor their flock and multiply the ministry of your church. 256 pgs.

CellChurch MAGAZINE
Cast the vision to every member of your church!
A CellChurch magazine in the hands of your church members every quarter will give them a clear understanding of your church's direction, values and vision.
(Discounts are available for bulk purchases) **Subscribe today!**

ORDER TOLL-FREE! 1-800-735-5865
Order Online: www.touchusa.org